A Quiet Moment in Time

A Contemporary View
of Amish Society

Other books by the authors
of *A Quiet Moment in Time—*

Lessons for Living
*A Practical Approach to Daily Life from
the Amish Community,*
by Joseph F. Donnermeyer, George M. Kreps,
and Marty W. Kreps

An Amish Winter Visit
A book for children
by Diane and Joseph Donnermeyer

A CONTEMPORARY VIEW OF AMISH SOCIETY

a Quiet Moment IN Time

George M. Kreps
Professor Emeritus
The Ohio State University

Joseph F. Donnermeyer
Professor
The Ohio State University

Marty W. Kreps
Honey Run Traditions
Frederick, Maryland

ISBN 1-890050-09-1

2673 T.R 421
Sugarcreek, OH 44681

Carlisle Printing
OF WALNUT CREEK ltd.

Foreword

"IF YOU ADMIRE OUR FAITH, STRENGTHEN YOURS"

Most tourists understand only a little about the Amish. What they can see, hear, and experience on their travels to an area where the Amish live provides a very incomplete snapshot. Sometimes the tourist businesses which claim to educate outsiders about the Amish, whether intentional or not, provide facts that only stereotype and give the wrong impression.

Readers should not view their lack of understanding with dismay. Most tourists spend only a few hours of a single day visiting an Amish area. How could anyone understand another culture in so short a time? After all, would we expect a person who visits the United States from another country for a few days to fully understand the American way of life?

Each year millions of tourists visit areas where the Amish live. The popularity of the Amish skyrocketed as America changed from a nation of small towns and family farms to a society of televisions, high technology, and urban sprawl, and many people desire a break from their fast-paced lifestyles. A drive in the country, a chance to do a little shopping, and the opportunity to see and learn about a people who have maintained their agrarian roots and rural lifestyle becomes almost irresistible. The Amish reputation for their resistance to owning and using many of the technologies that supposedly define modern life reminds tourists that there is more to living than climbing the corporate ladder and "keeping up with the Jone's."

Most tourists, however, learn amazingly little about the Amish. They may see a buggy on the road and hear the characteristic clip-clop of the horse's hooves. If they are lucky, they may have the chance to view an Amish man plowing a field with a team of Belgian or Percheron workhorses. Some tourists become particularly enthralled with Amish children, and will rush to take pictures even though the Amish strongly prefer that photographs not be taken because they believe it to be a violation of the Second Commandment (*"Thou shalt not make unto thee any graven image, or any likeness of any thing that is*

Most tourists see the Amish as a people who farm and live the "old-fashioned" way. What lies behind their selective use of modern technology and preference for a way of life based on religious values, is a contemporary prescription for living.

in heaven above, or that is in the earth beneath, or that is in the water under the earth" —Exodus 20:4).

But what has the tourist learned? As anyone who has ever lived in another country fully appreciates, to understand another culture can take years of direct experience living in the area, speaking the language of the people, eating the food they eat, and working side by side with them. It requires a total immersion.

A one-day visit to an Amish community is certainly not a total immersion, even if repeated a hundred times. However, the reader should take heart. There is still a great deal that can be learned about the Amish, and in so doing, that can be learned about oneself and about society in general.

Our goal is to help the visitor have an educational experience by providing a short, straightforward, and accurate description of the Amish, their history, and their culture. This book was written to improve the visitor's ability to understand what is seen, heard, and experienced, even if, as a tourist, the trip is short, and there is limited direct contact with the Amish. *The authors believe that the tourist experience is enhanced when tourists can see the connection between the history and religious heritage of the Amish, and the way they live today. No matter how peculiar or different the Amish may seem, what they do is based on their past and their sense of how they should maintain and pass on their religious values to future generations, and all the while living within a society, American society, which is it-*

self always changing.

This book also provides an introduction for the more serious reader. There are many scholarly books about the Amish, but these are often long and laborious for readers who are just starting their educational journeys. These readers should view this book as the beginning of the trail that leads to the more detailed scholarly accounts in other books, such as those listed at the end of this volume.

How does one learn? An open mind is one important condition. So too is a curiosity that motivates one to learn. One of our Amish friends referred us to a passage in an article written by an Amish man in the *Small Farmer's Journal* (Summer issue, 1993).

> "We realize that not everyone is cut out to be one of the plain people. Many have not the opportunity; but here is the challenge: If you admire our faith—strengthen yours. If you admire our sense of commitment—deepen yours. If you admire our community spirit, build your own. If you admire the simple life—cut back. If you admire deep character and enduring values, live them yourself."

The authors are hopeful that the readers of this book will heed these words, and that the words in this book will help them on their journeys toward an understanding of the Amish and, more importantly, of themselves.

George Kreps, Joseph Donnermeyer, and Marty Kreps became interested in the Amish culture when Marty began working with Amish women in Holmes County, Ohio who made quilts and handicrafts for her business. She visited in their homes, got to know their children, and even took an Amish woman to a quilt sale in California with her. A longtime friendship has since developed between the Amish and the authors. They have attended weddings, visited their schools, their farms, their businesses, and a barn raising. They have visited friends in Lancaster County, Pennsylvania, and several smaller settlements and have been able to make comparisons between the communities. Holmes County, Ohio, and Lancaster County, Pennsylvania, are the two largest of all Amish communitites. George was born and raised on a small farm in southeastern Pennsylvania near the Amish community in Lancaster County. His academic interests have been in theology, anthropology, and rural sociology. He is a Professor Emeritus at The Ohio State University, Agricultural Technical Institute in Wooster, Ohio, and is currently an adjunct professor at Frederick Community College in Maryland. He and Marty teach a course on "Amish Culture" and regularly conduct field trips to the Lancaster County area.

Joe was born and raised in northern Kentucky near Cincinnati. He is a professor of rural sociology at The Ohio State University in Columbus, Ohio. He annually teaches a course on "Amish Society" and was recently recognized by the university for teaching excellence. Joe and his wife, Diane (an elementary education teacher), have written a children's book titled *An*

Amish Winter Visit (Tater Ridge Press).

Marty grew up in rural southeastern Ohio. She is a graduate of The Ohio State University and has worked with social service agencies in Ohio, Maryland, and Alabama. She conducts interviews with Amish families in Ohio, Pennsylvania, and Maryland. She teaches workshops about the Amish and guides tour groups to Amish communities.

Over the years, we have made many Amish friends. We hope that you too enjoy the Amish as friends and neighbors.

⌒Acknowledgements⌒

The information for this book comes from many sources. It comes from the Amish themselves, especially those living in Holmes County, Ohio, and the surrounding counties of Coshocton, Stark, Tuscarawas, and Wayne. This is called the greater Holmes County community, and is the largest community of Amish worldwide. Second, information for this book comes from descriptions of the other large communities where the Amish live, including Lancaster County, Pennsylvania; Elkhart and LaGrange Counties, Indiana; and Geauga County, Ohio. Third, this book relies upon information and facts provided about the Amish by books, articles in scientific journals, and various newspaper and magazine accounts.

One newspaper that is very informative is *The Budget*. It is a local newspaper published out of Sugarcreek in Tuscarawas County. *The Budget* is a weekly newspaper that includes reports of local news about Amish and Mennonite communities sent in from all over North America. These letters frequently contain valuable lessons about life which we want to share with our readers, and are found at the beginning of each chapter.

Fourth, there are scholars familiar with the Amish who have shared their insights with us, such as Donald Kraybill, as well as John Hostetler and William Schreiber, both of whom are now deceased. We also want to acknowledge the support of the Heritage Historical Library in Alymer, Ontario, Elizabeth

Cooksey, Associate Professor in the Department of Sociology at The Ohio State University, Roger Williams, Professor of Entomology, Ohio Agricultural Research and Development Center, Wooster, Ohio, John Cochran, Akron, Ohio, and Nick Miller, Walnut Creek, Ohio.

And, of course, we want to acknowledge the comments and observations of the thousands of "students" of all ages who enrolled in our courses, participated in our workshops, and accompanied us on our tours. Finally, we want to thank those who read the transcripts of this book and offered their suggestions. Some of the pictures were taken by the authors, or provided by their friends and students.

Table Of Contents

A QUIET MOMENT IN TIME

1

The *Basics*

Ten
Important
Characteristics
About
The
Amish

"The corn has been harvested.
The yield is not as good as years before,
but the Bible says 'in everything
give thanks.' So we feel our needs were met."

The Budget, November 1996

⌒The Basics⌒

Have you ever wondered what it means to be an American? How about an Indonesian, an Italian, a Chinese, or a Kenyan? How would you answer someone from another country who asked you to describe several of the most important characteristics of American society?

Every society has a unique set of features, which are the core of that society. The Amish are part of American society, but at the same time, they are a distinctive group within it. What are the key features of Amish society, and what are those things that make them different from the rest of Americans?

On the following pages are ten important facts that describe these core features. They serve as the reader's introduction to the Amish—an introduction that the authors hope goes beyond the superficial impressions of the drive-by tourist.

One: Most Amish Breadwinners Work in Non-Farm Occupations

Historically, Amish have been farmers. About five hundred years ago in Europe, when the roots of the Amish faith began, most everyone was a farmer. They refer to the Old Testament passage from Genesis when God commanded Adam and Eve to "dress" and keep (cultivate) the garden.

In the greater Holmes County community of Northeast Ohio about one in every five Amish breadwinners primarily makes a living from agriculture. Farmland is expensive. Non-farm job opportunities mean that children can get married, start their own families, and still live near their parents and in-laws. So, the value of maintaining fellowship and face-to-face communication, and the development of many Amish-owned businesses has reduced their reliance on agriculture.

Many church elders and scholars who study the Amish see this trend as a serious threat to the core of Amish values and culture. That may be so, but even in Amish families where the breadwinner works in a factory, the woman of the house maintains a garden, and the Amish live in rural areas surrounded by farmland, and these help to maintain the Amish connection to the land.

The reader should remember that the Amish may have many traditions, but they are not old-fashioned. They are a diverse and dynamic society. They are changing all the time, and have always changed. That is because the world around them is always changing and presenting the Amish with new challenges. No religion, and no culture, can maintain its vitality without challenge and renewal. The history and heritage of the Amish will remain agricultural. However, someday it could be that the Amish will be completely out of farming and will find other ways of making a living while still adhering to their religious values and a lifestyle separate and distinctive from others around them.

Two: Selective Use of Technologies in the Home, on the Farm, and in Their Businesses

Most of these restrictions go back to the early 1900s, when some

These phone shanties are symbolic of how the Amish selectively allow aspects of modern technology into their society. The telephone booth on the left is for a family, and the one on the right is for use by the employees of a nearby sawmill.

Amish began to have phones installed, and Amish were purchasing cars. However, there was concern about adoption of these new inventions, especially in terms of their impact on Amish beliefs in maintaining themselves as a distinctive people. In addition, they were concerned that ownership and use of these new inventions would erode their desire to live together as a community of believers in the same religious values. Fellowship depends on face-to-face communication, and modern technology reduces the need to communicate this way. Later, similar debates occurred over the use of the radio and the television. In each case, the Amish have weighed the consequences and decided to turn down these technologies, although some compromises have been made.

The Amish have compromised on the use of the telephone. For example, many "telephone shanties" can be found on the back

Living in the midst of a society filled with cars, trucks, factories, tourists, and modern technology, the Ordnung helps maintain the fence that makes the Amish way of life distinctive.

roads in areas where the Amish live. These shanties are usually located at the end of the lane or across the street from the home, and the phone is owned by the Amish. The number is usually unlisted and use of the phone is restricted to making appointments and conducting business with non-Amish. Some Amish are now permitted to install a phone in the barn or in their shop, but restrictions on its use remain. Some Amish now have cell phones, which present new challenges to maintaining a strong sense of community.

Although Amish do not permit their members to use electricity from the public power lines, they have made many compromises here as well. For example, Amish will use batteries for starting stationary engines, and for running adding machines, calculators, clocks, flashlights, and other workshop and household items. Many Amish businesses use large diesel engines for lighting and to run hydraulic and pneumatic power tools and machinery. Amish who work for "English" employers work in environments where electricity is used every day. Debate about situations in which electricity is or is not allowed continues to this day among members and leaders of the church districts.

The Amish refer to non-Amish as the **"English"** because it is the language used by everyone else around them. The English language itself has many of its roots in the German language, and many words from both languages sound the same and mean the same thing. In addition, sentence structure and grammar are somewhat alike. This allows tourist businesses to pick Amish-sounding German words that tourists can recognize, such as restaurants that use the word "Haus" for House.

Three: *Ordnung* and *Meidung*

One very important concept that will help the reader to understand the Amish is the *Ordnung* (pronounced ott-ning). Many tourists and people who know only a little about the Amish see only that they dress differently, do not drive cars, and do not use electricity or have telephones in their homes. There is much more, and it is reflected in the *Ordnung*.

Ordnung is both a set of rules and regulations for living and a confession of the Amish faith. It can be described as "the fence" that distinguishes between those in fellowship with the Amish faith and all others.

The Amish are organized into church districts, each composed of several dozen families headed by a group of elders including a bishop, two ministers, and one deacon. Each church district has its own *Ordnung* or rules for living. That is why different groups of Amish do things differently. For example, some Amish drive buggies that have no rearview mirrors. Others have rearview mirrors, but paint the chrome around the mirror black. Still others have rearview mirrors and do not paint the chrome. In all Amish church districts, the *Ordnung* is constantly examined, and the church leaders, along with all adult baptized members, discuss the rules and both reaffirm those that need not change, and change those that need an adjustment.

There is much variety in the Amish *Ordnung*. The Amish are like the quilts they make, each patch may be different, but the Amish are sewn together by their common history and religious values. There is one other thing important for the reader to know about the *Ordnung*; it is largely oral, and only a few parts of it are written down.

Meidung (pronounced mide-ung) or shunning means cutting off fellowship with and avoiding former members who have been excommunicated, that is, told to leave the Amish faith because of the seriousness of their transgressions against the *Ordnung*. Only adults who have been baptized Amish are subject to the *Meidung*. *Meidung* is almost exclusively used for the punishment of sins not relating to the *Ordnung*, but for sins as described in the Bible.

Meidung or shunning is probably the least understood, and yet one of the most fascinating aspects of Amish society for outsiders. The reasons for the imposition of shunning can vary between progressive and conservative Amish groups, but it is not exercised lightly or arbitrarily. *Meidung* is the last effort to bring about a change in the behavior of one of their members and is the will of the members and church leaders.

All of their lives, the Amish are taught the expectations and consequences of breaking the *Ordnung*. When Amish boys and girls grow up, they are certainly encouraged, but not forced, to be baptized and join the church. Once they make this decision, they are bound by the rules of the church (the *Ordnung*), and there are dire and well-defined consequences if the rules are not followed. The Amish feel that rules are necessary to maintain standards. The church leaders have worked with the individual over a long period of time and feel that they have no other recourse in order to maintain the continuity of the church and of the *Ordnung*. It is a sad time for everyone when the ban is imposed because the individual is separated from family, friends, and church. Shunning is considered the last resort, the culmination of a series of failed attempts at reconciliation with the *Ordnung* of the church district. If the person sincerely repents, fellowship will again be restored.

The *Meidung* presents difficult choices for families when one of their members is excommunicated. Parents want to be able to stay in touch with an adult son or daughter who has been shunned. Sometimes a whole family will leave the church district rather than shun one of their own.

Disagreements about the use of *Meidung* has contributed to

numerous divisions of the Amish since their original split from the Mennonites in 1693. More conservative interpretations of the *Meidung* would dictate that all association with former members is stopped. More liberal interpretations view shunning as less than all-inclusive and not forever. For example, once an excommunicated member has joined another church, perhaps another Amish group, a Mennonite group, or other Protestant denominations, then communication may be permitted again.

Four: *Gelassenheit*

Gelassenheit (pronounced gay las en hite) means yielding to a higher authority. This concept represents the general attitude of the Amish toward living. The Amish believe in living a life of humility and submission to God, as well as the church district's leaders and *Ordnung*. The excerpt from *The Budget* at the beginning of this chapter represents an example of *Gelassenheit*. The harvest was less than expected, but "needs were met" because the "Bible says 'in everything give thanks.'"

Gelassenheit helps us to understand why owning and using so many modern conveniences and technology is restricted or forbidden by the *Ordnung*. However, *Gelassenheit* is much more. It represents expectations for the appropriate way to speak and to behave, such as not drawing attention to one's self through verbal boasting or nonconforming dress. Boys and girls are taught these things from the crib until the time they, as adults, choose to be baptized, and it is reinforced for them as adults until the day they die. It symbolizes a church of members in close-knit fellowship, who continuously discuss issues of faith and ways they should lead their lives.

Five: Conducting Church Services in Homes Rather Than in Church Buildings

One of the characteristics that distinguishes the Amish from all other Christian denominations is that they conduct their church service in members' houses. The Sunday service rotates from one residence to another. Eventually, except under special circumstances, everyone's home in a church district will host the service at least once each year. For a typical church district, hosting a service means having 200 or more people coming to the house. Both adults and children attend the service.

Services begin about 8:30-9:00 a.m. and are quite long—about 3¹/₂ hours. A meal, which has been prepared by the host family, follows the service and afterwards people stay to talk and visit until it is time to go home for the late afternoon and evening chores.

Six: Distinctive Use of Pennsylvania Dutch for Daily Language and High German for Church Services

Pennsylvania Dutch or German is the language spoken at home by the Amish. The use of Pennsylvania Dutch helps the Amish define their world and maintain their distinctiveness. It reminds them of their origins from German-speaking areas of Europe, and it reminds them that they are a separate people who follow their particular way to observe their Christian faith.

Why is it called Pennsylvania Dutch? Originally it was a dialect spoken by Germans who had moved to south central and south-western Pennsylvania. Although English speakers use the word "German," the German equivalent is "Deutsche," which sounds similar to the English word "Dutch." Gradually, over time, the dialect became known as Pennsylvania Dutch.

Few persons outside of the Amish and Conservative Mennonites speak Pennsylvania Dutch today. In Amish society, the Pennsylvania Dutch dialect is the language of work, family, friendship, play, and intimacy. Young children live largely in the world of this dialect until they go to school and begin to learn English. By the end of the eighth grade, Amish boys and girls have learned their second language of English, and communicate using English with their non-Amish neighbors. However, when speaking among themselves, the Amish mostly use Pennsylvania Dutch, but often will mix in English phrases.

An Amish version of standard German is used for religious purposes. The Bible is read in the *High German*, as are other books and writings of a religious nature. They are fluent in two languages (English and Pennsylvania Dutch) and use high German for their church services.

Seven: Distinctive Manner of Dress

One of the questions frequently asked is: why do the Amish dress the way they do? There are several parts to the answer. In the first place, it is traditional; dress represents continuity with the past. Second, distinctive dress represents a way for the Amish to maintain a feeling of group identity. Plainness and modesty in dress is a way for them to practice nonconformity or separate-ness from the world (Romans 12:1 & 2). Third, distinctive dress gives testimony to their faith because it sets them apart.

Like the "English," the Amish have different types of clothes for different occasions. For the Amish, dress is simpler and is of

The distinctiveness of Amish dress serves as a symbol of separation from the "English" world.

three types: for work, social activities, and church.

The girls dress like their mothers and the boys dress like their fathers. Women wear a covering on their head at all times. This is called a prayer covering. Even little girls as young as six weeks old wear a head covering. The covering is a symbol of submission to God and His structure of authority. Their dresses are plain-colored material. Print material is frowned upon. Women, both young and old, wear an apron.

At her wedding, a bride wears a white cape and apron, symbols of virginity. The wedding dress, always hand made, is usually a shade of blue. Both single and married women wear a white cape and apron to church all their lives. The colored cape and apron will be worn at most other functions, and is usually the same color as the dress.

Mothers outfit their baby boys with pants during the fifth month. At about four years of age, the boys start wearing an adult-styled suit which includes a vest, suspenders, coat, hat, and "broadfall" trousers. Men shave until marriage, after which time they wear a beard. In some ways this serves in lieu of a wedding band. The men wear a distinctive broad-brimmed hat. The hat is worn whenever a male is outside the house.

The *Ordnung* of various church districts will allow for variations in dress. For example, men and women from more conservative Amish church districts restrict themselves mostly to darker clothes. More progressive districts, while still maintaining plain dress, will allow lighter colors.

Eight: The Use of Horses and Buggies

The horse and buggy is a significant outer symbol of Amish religious values and distinctive lifestyle. The silhouette of a horse and buggy is also the most frequently used illustration on billboards, signs, and ads to promote tourism.

The Amish have two main uses for horses and each requires a different type of horse. Standardbred horses pull the buggies used for transportation. These horses are bought from racehorse

Like dress, horses are a symbol of leading a life that is different. The use of horses allows the Amish to live closer to each other, where they are better able to reinforce their religious values through face-to-face interaction.

owners. These racehorses are not good enough for racing or have become too old to race. Draft horses are used on the farm for plowing, disking, planting, harvesting, and other field work. They are usually Belgians or Percherons, relatives to the Clydesdale horses that are more familiar to the general public.

A buggy horse normally costs about $3,000-$4,000, although some can go much higher. Draft horses can cost a little bit less. Both buggy and draft horses have a useful life span of about 15 years. Like most horse owners, each horse is given a name, and this name is used when directions are given to the horse.

Horses are not only important symbols for a distinctive way of life, they reinforce *Gelassenheit*. They can usually travel about 10 miles in an hour, so the Amish tend to cluster in a relatively small area so that they can visit each other and it is not an unreasonable distance to go for church services.

There are several types of buggies and carriages used by the Amish. In addition to the standard carriage, which is most frequently seen by tourists, there is the open buggy, the spring wagon, the market wagon, and the two-wheeled cart. The market wagon can be seen on the roads during market and auction days in country towns in Amish areas.

Horses limit the size of a farming operation. Farms normally are between 50 and 150 acres in size. However, using horses has certain advantages. Farmers can get to their fields earlier in the spring with horses than with tractors. This is an advantage in years with wet spring weather. A horse does not compact the soil like tractors and combines, so the soil on Amish farms is more productive, and, of course, horses are a source of free fertilizer.

Many Amish own tractors, but they do not use them for field work. Instead, they use tractors for "belt power," somewhat akin to a mobile gasoline engine used for running stationary equipment and for moving heavy objects around the barn.

Businesses with Amish customers have special places with hitching rails for parking buggies. In the larger settlements of Amish, some fast-food restaurants, banking institutions, and department chain stores have installed hitching rails in order to accommodate their Amish customers.

Frequently, the Amish will hire a van from an "English" neighbor or friend for longer distance travel or when traveling in larger groups. Also, employers provide a van for transporting their Amish workers to and from their homes.

Nine: Ways in Which Amish and Mennonites Differ

The Amish are a different group from the Mennonites, but share the same roots. Both groups are variations of Christianity and both are part of a branch of Protestantism that is known as Anabaptism. The Anabaptist movement began in 1525 and emphasized the importance of adult baptism. Anabaptist means to be "rebaptized," and refers to the belief that infant baptism, which was the common practice among both Catholics and many of the newly formed Protestant groups of the time, does not follow the teachings of Christ; therefore, they were rebaptized.

Early in their history, the Anabaptists became known as the **Mennonites** due to the influence of a former Dutch Catholic priest named **Menno Simons**, who joined the Anabaptist movement soon after its start. His writings helped define the religious values of the Anabaptists.

The **Amish** started in **1693** over a dispute about a number of religious issues (see the next chapter on the history of the Amish). The Amish were named for their leader, **Jacob Ammann**. He led a group that split from the Mennonites–Swiss Brethren because they felt that the Mennonites–Swiss Brethren had become too worldly.

Today, there is a great deal of variation within both the Amish and Mennonite faiths. It is difficult to say that all Amish are one way, and all Mennonites are a different way. Keeping this in mind, however, it can be said that in general, the Amish are more conservative than the Mennonites. The Amish have been more conscientious about keeping their religion and their over-all life-style distinctive from the rest of American society. Mennonites are less conservative than the Amish and are closer to mainline Protestant denominations, and their lifestyle is more similar to mainstream American life. For example, the Mennonites have church buildings, while the Amish do not, as mentioned earlier. Amish are stricter than Mennonites about members associating with those who have dropped out or been excommunicated from the Amish faith. Most Amish do not have Sunday school, and many Mennonite congregations do. Amish restrict their use of technology, maintain traditional dress, and a greater share of Amish make their living from farming. Although some conservative Mennonite groups lead a similar lifestyle, most do not. Mennonites own and drive cars and those who farm use tractors for field work. In addition, most Mennonites do not wear traditional clothes.

Ten: Growth and Expansion

The Amish double their population every 20 to 25 years. That's a phenomenal rate of population growth! The reason is simple. The Amish have large families and see children as a "blessing from God." Plus, most girls and boys decide to be baptized Amish when they are young adults, and remain Amish for the rest of their lives. To accommodate this growth, the number of new communities is increasing rapidly, with 10 to 15 established each year.

2

History of the

Amish

"June 1991 marks the 150th anniversary
of the first Amish to settle in the state of Indiana.
In 1841 four families came from Somerset County, PA.
The year before, in 1840, four men…
started out on a western trip, 'land shopping'…
Consequently, the next spring 4 young families got
ready to move. No doubt there was a lot of excitement,
also some mixed feelings. Pulling up roots
that are deep is not an easy matter."

The Budget, July 1991

⌒ History of the Amish ⌒

Many people travel to places where they have an opportunity to learn about a culture or society other than their own. What they witness can be considered strange and bewildering by their own standards. This is often the case with travelers to Amish country. One way to understand all societies, including the Amish, is to understand their history. A people's history is their roots, and as anyone who grows a garden knows, without roots plants cannot establish themselves and grow, and propagate the next generation of plants.

The Amish are a branch of Christianity that began in Europe soon after the Protestant Reformation. Catholicism had been the dominant religion in Europe for over 1,000 years, but corruption and scandal had caused many to question the central authority of the Papacy. Of course, the best known of the protesters was Martin Luther, but there were many others, including Huldreich Zwingli in Zurich, Switzerland.

Luther, Zwingli, and others drew many distinctions between themselves and Catholicism, but they had two things in common with the Catholic Church of that time. **First**, there was no separation of church and state. As Protestantism and Catholicism competed for religious as well as political dominance, the various kingdoms and principalities across Europe would choose one side or the other, and expect all of their subjects to conform. **Sec-**

ond, the Catholic Church and nearly all of the various Protestant groups accepted the idea of "infant baptism." In other words, a baby born to a family living in an area where the nobility sided with the Protestants or the Catholics, was baptized a Protestant or a Catholic. There was no choice in the matter.

Both of these practices were the source of dissent for a new group of reformers in and around Zurich, who believed that government sponsorship of religion and infant baptism were contrary to the teachings of Christ in the New Testament. They believed that faith transformed the believer into a follower of Christ.

The followers of Zwingli and the Zurich Council considered these protesters to be "radicals" and dangerous to the state. The formal break came on **January 21, 1525**, when the protesters symbolically rebaptized themselves. **Anabaptist** means to be rebaptized and this was the original name given to the group. Almost immediately, and for the next two hundred years, Anabaptists were hunted down, martyred, thrown off their land, and harassed in other ways by many Protestant groups and Catholics alike. Thousands died, and during their early years, meetings and religious services were conducted secretly in the woods and in caves. This set the stage for the Amish tradition of holding their services at their homes.

Some Anabaptist groups came to be known as the **Mennonites** because one of their early leaders was a former Catholic priest from the Netherlands named **Menno Simons** (1496-1561). His leadership and writings were very influential in helping to define the beliefs and practices of these rebaptizers.

The intense persecution left lasting marks. One book, first published in 1660 and still read today, is called the *Martyr's Mirror*. It includes hundreds of stories of martyrdom, as well as the basic tenets of the Anabaptists.

A belief that emerged among the Anabaptists was an emphasis on separation, that is, dividing the world into believers and nonbelievers. They cited St. Paul's Epistle to the Romans (12:2) which says *"Be not conformed to this world, but*

Menno Simons joined the Anabaptist movement soon after it began, and was one of the first to write about Anabaptist beliefs.

The Martyr's Mirror is a book about the persecution of Anabaptists in Europe. This picture shows an 1870 German-language edition. The Martyr's Mirror is still read by Amish, and many Mennonites as well.

be ye transformed by the renewing of your mind..."; and Corinthians II (6:14), which emphasized *"Be ye not unequally yoked together with unbelievers: for what fellowship hath righteousness with unrighteousness? and what communion hath light with darkness."* Shunning, or avoiding contact with former believers who were excommunicated, became an accepted practice.

Many Mennonites–Swiss Brethren took up farming and animal husbandry, especially in the areas of the Jura Mountains of Switzerland and the Vosges Mountains of the present-day French province of Alsace. Others lived in the Palatinate region of Germany and further north in the Netherlands, and as well, in other places throughout Europe. Scholars today agree that the two main groups of Mennonites were the Swiss Mennonites (Swiss Brethren) and the Dutch Mennonites. It was from the Swiss Mennonite branch that the Amish Church was formed.

Life continued to be hard for the Mennonites through the 16th and 17th centuries as persecution and wars forced hardships on many. Despite this, over the years Mennonites were often given aid by many local people who were not Anabaptist. They were called the **true-hearted or *"treuherzige"*** people. Mennonite groups in Switzerland, where persecution remained harsher than among Mennonite groups living further north, relied on the *treuherzige* in order to survive.

Eventually, the relationship between Mennonites and other religious groups created a problem among those who took a stricter interpretation of Anabaptist beliefs about separation from the world and of too much fellowship with non-believers, that is, those who were not Mennonites. A church elder by the name of **Jacob Ammann** (c. 1656–c. 1730), and those who agreed with him, had become concerned about what they believed to be a weakening of Anabaptist beliefs and laxity of practices. Part of the controversy focused on association with and accepting help from the *treuherzige*. Another point of contention was over communion. Ammann and others believed that communion should be given twice a year, rather than once, because it was important for renewal of the faith. They also placed greater importance on foot-washing, in accordance with the Gospel, during the service when communion is given.

Many of the principal historic events described in these pages surrounding the Anabaptist movement in Europe occurred in the Rhine River provinces of present-day France and Germany, and in the countries of Switzerland and the Netherlands.

After a series of meetings and failed attempts to reconcile differences between the two sides during the summer months of 1693, the groups went their separate ways. In fact, the elders of both groups excommunicated each other. Followers of the more conservative group led by Jacob Ammann came to be known as the **Amish.**

Conditions in Europe at the time, including war, poverty, and lack of religious freedom, made the English colonies in America attractive to both the Amish and the Mennonites. By the 1720s, Mennonites, and a little later, the Amish, began relocating to eastern Pennsylvania, influenced by William Penn, who traveled the Rhine River valley, recruiting persecuted groups for his colony in America. The first record of Amish immigration to the American colonies was in 1737, when a few families came over on a boat called the *Charming Nancy.*

The Amish first settled in Berks and Lancaster Counties of Pennsylvania. Today Lancaster County is the location of the second largest group of Amish, and is the oldest of all the communities. Immigration of Amish continued through the remainder of the 1700s and up to about 1860, although a few families also migrated to America as late as 1880.

A **little known fact** is that there are no Amish remaining in Europe. Amish groups who stayed in Europe continued to suffer from conditions of persecution and many political and economic hardships during the eighteenth and nineteenth centuries. Finding land where Amish families could be close to one another in order to maintain fellowship with each other and attend Sunday services was difficult. Eventually, those Amish who stayed behind became assimilated into local Mennonite and various Protestant denominations.

The right to own land, and the ample supply of newly opened frontier land, along with strong beliefs in fellowship and separation from the world, were key factors in helping the Amish flourish in America. As the United States expanded westward, so too did the Amish. Today, the Amish continue to establish new settlements as they find ways to maintain their religious values in times of rapid technological, economic, and social change.

The history of the Amish in America is not always a story of "smooth sailing." They have confronted and found solutions to many issues that challenged their beliefs in a life of separation, cooperation, and humility. For example, during the 1860s, another great debate occurred between elders who espoused change and church leaders who held more firmly for tradition. Almost annually, from 1862 to 1878, a series of *Diener-Versammlungen* or **ministers' meetings** were held, mostly in Holmes and Wayne Counties in Ohio, Elkhart and LaGrange Counties in Indiana (which is today the location of the third largest Amish community); and Mifflin County, Pennsylvania. The division was over religious values and interpretations of adopting a lifestyle that was considered modern for that period of time. But the division was also a geographic division. The progressives were primarily from the newer communities in states west of the Mississippi River. The conservatives were mostly from the older communities to the east.

As in 1693, another great schism occurred. The more conservative Amish groups came to be known as the **Old Order**, while the more progressive groups were originally called **Amish-Mennonites**. Eventually, the various Amish-Mennonite groups dropped the word "Amish" from the name of their denominations and conferences, and today are considered Mennonite.

More schisms occurred during the twentieth century, and in every case, the differences concerned disagreements over religious values and lifestyle. However, in many cases, the groups who have split off from the Old Order Amish have maintained their identity as Amish, but are of a different fellowship. For example, in the greater Holmes County community, besides the Old Order Amish who make up about 75 percent of the Amish population, there are three other affiliations of Amish. Lining up all four affiliations, from the conservative to the progressive, these affiliations are known by the names **Swartzentruber Amish, Andy Weaver Amish, Old Order Amish, and New Order Amish**. These groups differ on many issues, including appropriate dress, use of farm and shop machinery, indoor and outdoor plumbing and other household conveniences, safety devices on buggies, and conditions under which members may interact with the non-Amish.

Since coming to America, the Amish have made a simple distinction between themselves and the non-Amish. Although some non-Amish neighbors may know the **Pennsylvania Dutch** dialect that the Amish use when they communicate with each other, 99.9 plus percent of non-Amish do not (some Mennonites do speak **Pennsylvania Dutch**, too). So the Amish refer to everyone else as the **"English"** because it is the dominant language in the United States and Canada.

During the twentieth century, the history of the Amish has been one of keeping many aspects of the "English" world at bay as the United States and Canada urbanized and technological developments changed the people of both countries. The ownership and use of electricity, television, telephones, cars, tractors, and other technologies that the "English" take for granted, have been carefully debated and considered by the Amish in terms of their impact on Amish faith and values.

World War I and II also presented challenges to Amish beliefs in pacifism. This pacifism grew from New Testament passages on separation from nonbelievers, and from their experiences with wars and persecution in Europe. Historical accounts indicate that a few Amish served in the military during the Revolutionary and Civil Wars, and other Amish sold supplies to the military. However, for the most part, they have stayed clear of military service and involvement and held fast to their pacifism.

The World Wars created difficult conditions for the Amish. **First,** the Amish spoke a dialect of German and were identified as having Germanic roots. Pacifism did not sit well with many "English" who viewed it as an action sympathetic to Germany. **Second,** military conscription meant that many young Amish men would be drafted. The Amish, along with other "peace churches," including the Mennonites, Brethren, and Quakers, lobbied the government for conscientious objector status and alternative service. In addition, many Amish were granted deferred status as "agricultural workers."

Alternative service created another challenge for the Amish. It meant that young men were sent to civilian public service camps. Church elders worried that many would not be able to keep their faith in these camps, and that they would fall prey to the temptations of the outside world. In general, most young men kept their Amish faith. The Amish maintained their pacifism during the Korean and Vietnam Wars, and once again, many young Amish men served alternative service.

A second challenge in this century was **compulsory education**. In the early part of the twentieth century, Amish children went to school with English children. At the time, rural schools were mostly simple one-room structures holding all eight grades, and most children did not go on to high school. The school year was built around farm work, which was always the first priority. As the country industrialized, the demands for a more skilled work force increased. States began to pass laws requiring young people to attend schools through the twelfth grade. Schools consolidated, and new subject matter was adopted which appeared to have no practical value for an Amish way of life.

As early as 1914 in Geauga County, Ohio (which is the location today of the fourth largest community of Amish), Amish parents were fined if their children did not attend school until the age of 16. Over the next several decades, officials in many states tried various ways of enforcing rules on compulsory education. However, the issue was important to the Amish because they believe that children should learn only the practical skills needed for their way of life. The rest was "higher education" that was unnecessary. Furthermore, Amish values on separation from the world were not compatible with consolidated schools and the idea of Amish children mixing with non-Amish children, especially during teenage years when decisions to be baptized Amish and to marry Amish were made.

In various ways, the Amish resisted compulsory education. Many parents held their children back so that they did not complete the eighth grade until they were older, and others had their children repeat the eighth grade. Some parents were fined or held briefly in prison. On Friday, November 19, 1965, in **Hazleton, Iowa**, county officials showed up at an Amish school to

As their population has grown, so too has the number of Amish parochial schools.

take the children by bus to a nearby public school. The children were brought out of the Amish school, but ran into an adjoining cornfield, where most of them successfully hid from officials. A photograph of the children fleeing toward the field appeared in many newspapers across the country. It did not look good for the county officials. The resulting publicity prompted the Governor of Iowa to issue a moratorium against further actions on compulsory education for the Amish.

A case originating in Green County, Wisconsin, ended up settling the issue. Local officials there accused Amish fathers of violating compulsory education laws. These men were found guilty. As was the case in Europe, so too in America there have always been many non-Amish who provide assistance to the Amish, especially when the issues center on American values of religious freedom. A Lutheran minister from Michigan by the name of William Lindholm, who was a native of Iowa and who had followed the incident in Hazleton, and William Ball, an attorney from Pennsylvania, spearheaded an effort to appeal the Green County decision. They were unsuccessful in overturning the verdict at the District Court level, but eventually convinced the U.S. Supreme Court to review the decision. On May 15, 1972, the Supreme Court ruled that constitutional rights of separation of church and state guaranteed the Amish exemption from compulsory education. This famous case is known today as **Wisconsin versus Yoder.**

These and other incidents motivated the Amish to establish their own parochial schools. Amish schools number in the hundreds today. Wherever there are Amish, there can be found simple, wooden one-room schools, usually with outhouses marked "boys" and "girls," a swing set and a ball diamond for playing softball. Tourists driving by these schools should understand that they are not looking at a throwback to bygone days. **In fact, most of these schools are less than 40 years old.** These schools are symbols of Amish success in maintaining their basic values.

The Amish continue to address new issues that, from their point of view, hinder their ability to pursue a lifestyle that is consistent with their religious beliefs. For example, Amish who are self-employed or who work in a business owned by an Amish person are exempt from paying Social Security tax. The Amish belief in separation does not allow them to collect Social Security, and they are mostly self-insured for medical expenses. To participate in Social Security and other forms of insurance is to be too connected to the world.

Tourism and traffic, employment in "English"-owned businesses and factories, health and workplace safety regulations, and state regulations on the temperature of milk used for cheese production, and the use of the orange slow-moving vehicle signs on the back of buggies, are but a few of the challenges which the Amish face today. However, it should be remembered that the trials presented by the modern world are useful to the Amish, because they help make visible the boundaries between themselves and the "English."

The Amish have come a long way in their 300-year history.

No longer do the Amish suffer the persecution of past centuries. No longer are they hunted down and martyred as enemies of the state; but, the challenges of maintaining their identity as Amish, and the religious values to which they adhere, are a constant part of their lives.

Twenty Important Events in the History of the Amish

1. January 21, 1525: The **Anabaptist** (i.e., to be rebaptized) movement begins near Zurich, Switzerland, when a group opposed to state sponsorship of religion meets and the members are rebaptized.

2. February 1527: A group of leaders of the new Anabaptist movement meet near the border of Switzerland and Germany in the village of Schleitheim. Seven principles of the Anabaptist faith are agreed upon: adult baptism, shunning or the ban, communion, separation, leading lives as shepherds of Christ, pacifism, and the rejection of oaths. These came to be known as the **Schleitheim Confession of Faith.**

3. 1534: A group of Anabaptists, believing the second coming of Christ to be imminent, captured the city of Munster in Germany by force of arms. A year later they were defeated by a combined military force of Catholics and Protestants. The Anabaptist use of arms and their subsequent defeat at Munster was renounced by **Menno Simons,** who was influential in writing down the beliefs of the Anabaptist movement. In time, many of the Anabaptist groups came to be known as the Mennonites.

4. 1535: A group of Anabaptists were imprisoned at Passau, which is near the border between Germany and Austria. While in

prison, they wrote 53 hymns about sorrow, suffering, and salvation. By 1564 these and additional hymns were in print and are still sung today in Amish church services. The book of hymns is known as the *Ausbund*.

5. 1632: A conference held in Dordrecht in the Netherlands listed 18 articles of the Mennonite faith, re-emphasizing and expanding on the Schleitheim Confession. Today these articles are called the **Dordrecht Confession of Faith**.

6. 1660: The *Martyr's Mirror*, an account of religious persecution and martyrdom among the Anabaptists, is published. It is still read by the Amish and many Mennonites today.

7. Summer, 1693: **Jacob Ammann** and his followers break off from more progressive Swiss Brethren (Mennonites) over issues of communion, foot-washing, shunning, and fellowship with nonbelievers. This group became known as the Amish.

8. 1737: The first group of Amish immigrants to America came over on the ship *Charming Nancy*.

9. 1760: The **Conestoga** congregation of Amish in Lancaster County was the first permanent community and still exists today. The second largest group of Amish is located in Lancaster County, with a current estimated population of slightly over 22,000.

10. 1808: Amish began to settle in Holmes County and the surrounding counties of northeast Ohio. Known as the greater **Holmes County community**, it is now the largest among 350 plus Amish communities in the United States and Canada. Its present population is estimated at about 30,000.

11. 1848: The **Elkhart–LaGrange County, Indiana,** community is founded. This is the third largest Amish community today. Today, its population is about 18,000.

12. 1862-1878: The *Diener-Versammlungen (or ministers' meetings)* causes a split between the conservatives, now known as the **Old Order Amish,** and the progressives, who were originally called **Amish Mennonites,** but who have since dropped "Amish" from the name of their denominations.

13. 1886: The **Geauga County, Ohio,** community is begun. It is now the fourth largest community of Amish, with an estimated population of about 8,000.

14. 1913: A group known today as the **Swartzentruber Amish** broke away from the Old Order Amish. The Swartzentruber group believed the Old Order group to be too progressive.

15. World War I and II: The Amish reach special accommodations with the U.S. government on the issues of **conscientious objector status** and **alternative service.**

16. 1952: Another group of conservative Amish, called the **Andy Weaver** group, broke off from the Old Order Amish.

17. 1967-1969: A new affiliation of Amish which is today known as the **New Order Amish,** broke away from the Old Order group over religious and lifestyle issues. This group is considered more liberal in its adaptation and use of modern technology, but more conservative in its interpretation of the Bible. They believe that an individual can have knowledge of salvation through personal conversion, and practice the use of Sunday school. They are one of four major affiliations or fellowships of Amish found in the

greater Holmes County community.

18. November 19, 1965 and May 15, 1972: Near Hazleton, Iowa, a group of Amish children hide in a cornfield in order to avoid being bused to a public school. This incident and decades long resistance to **compulsory education** eventually resulted in a Supreme Court **exemption** for the Amish. Today, most Amish children attend parochial schools supported by Amish congregations.

19. 1965: Congress grants the Amish an exemption from paying Social Security taxes as a rider to a Medicare bill, except when they are working for a non-Amish employer. The Amish belief in separation does not allow them to collect Social Security upon retirement.

20. 1990: The United States Supreme Court overturns a Minnesota State Supreme Court decision which compelled the Amish to place **slow-moving vehicle** (SMV) signs on the backs of their buggies. However, other states continue to pursue legislation mandating SMVs on buggies, and most Amish, except for those who belong to the most conservative affiliations, use SMV signs on their buggies in the interest of safety. Other disagreements between the Amish and government regulations continue to this day, such as the objection by some Amish to wearing orange when hunting, health regulations on septic systems, and safety regulations in Amish-owned sawmills and other businesses.

3

Amish

Church

Life

"The highlight of last weekend was the wedding…
Attendance at the wedding
was around 225 guests which swelled
our Sunday morning service the next day."

The Budget, January 1994

⌒Amish Church Life⌒

merica is an incredibly diverse society in terms of religion. It is almost unique among the countries of the world both for the protection to worship freely that is provided by the Constitution and for the large number of religious groups who exercise this right.

Religion can be defined as a set of beliefs about God and salvation. The word **"church"** has two meanings. It refers both to a **group** of people who share and practice the same religious beliefs and to a **building** where people go to practice their religious rituals. No church building can be found among the Amish, for they hold their services in their homes. This makes them distinctive from almost all other Christian denominations, as well as from the various other religious groups that are free to practice their faith in America.

For the Amish, church life is nothing more and nothing less than living every day according to their values and beliefs. Every Amish community consists of one or more church districts. A church district normally consists of about 20 to 35 families. Church services are held every two weeks on Sunday (New Order Amish hold weekly services), and are rotated among the houses of church members.

Many religions have detailed church law, which is sometimes called ecclesiastical law. These rules are written down and are often quite lengthy and difficult for ordinary members to understand. Religious leaders come together in meetings to debate these laws and amend them when necessary. In contrast to all of this, Amish have fewer written laws. Most of what would be their church law is oral tradition passed down from generation to generation called the *Ordnung*.

Unlike many other religions, the Amish do not have much of a church hierarchy. Every church district has a bishop, two ministers, and one deacon. In addition, the bishops from various districts will come together, usually about once a year, to discuss issues of common concern.

Church Leaders

There are three types of church leaders in Amish church districts. The bishop is known as the *Völliger Diener* or "Full Servant." There is only one bishop for each church district, although sometimes there are two, when one of the bishops, who is considered retired, is not able to carry out his duties due to health reasons. The role of the bishop is to provide spiritual leadership and to be the spiritual head of the church district. The bishop preaches on Sunday, and performs baptisms, marriages, ordinations, and funerals. The bishop also pronounces excommunication (and the restoration of excommunicated members) when a case arises of serious violations of the *Ordnung*. However, the whole congregation votes on cases of excommunication and restoration.

The deacon is called the *Armendiener* or "Servant of the Poor."

Most church districts have one deacon, although a few have two. One of the deacon's major responsibilities is the physical welfare of the congregation. The deacon receives donated funds and distributes those funds according to need. Sometimes the collection is for the medical bills or problems of a family from another district. The deacon also reads assigned chapters from the Bible during the church service and assists the bishop in baptisms, communion, and matters of church discipline.

Diener Zum Buch or "Servant of the Book" is the name of the minister. Most Amish church districts have two ministers. The minister assists in the preaching at church services, along with the bishop, and help in providing guidance for the spiritual direction of the church district and its members.

Major Fellowships

Amish church districts usually identify with one of the affiliations or "Orders" that are the result of internal divisions into conservative and progressive branches. As the brief history of the Amish indicated, there was a major division in the 1860s, and the more traditional group became known at that time as the **Old Order Amish**. This group can be considered the mainstream group today because it is the largest of all. For example, in the greater Holmes County community, the Old Order Amish represent about 75 percent of all Amish. They form an even larger presence in the Lancaster County, Pennsylvania, and the Elkhart–LaGrange, Indiana, communities, and are the only fellowships in almost all the smaller communities. However, there are three other major affiliations.

The most conservative of the major affiliations is the **Swartz-entruber Amish**. The Swartzentruber Amish split from the Old Order Amish in about 1913 over how strictly shunning *(Meidung)* should be carried out. The Swartzentruber Amish are known today because they are also the most traditional in their refusal to use most forms of modern technology in the home and on the farm. They reject the use of the slow-moving vehicle signs on their buggies, and their buggies do not have rearview mirrors or a front windshield above the dash to help keep out the cold in winter. Innovations adopted by other Amish are not used by the Swartzentruber Amish, including indoor bathrooms, window blinds, a gas or kerosene refrigerator, and linoleum floors. However, gas-powered washing machines are approved. They will not use a tractor for any reason, and only stationary gas engines mounted on a wooden frame are used to help with the farm work. If a Swartzentruber Amish man does not make a living from farming, he will work for an Amish employer with the permission of the bishop. However, there are certain things he might not be allowed to do. The authors know of one Amish-owned business where most of the employees are Swartzentruber Amish, except for one person from a more progressive order of Amish, who operates the forklift.

The Andy Weaver Amish split with the Old Order Amish over, once again, the issue of shunning. The Old Order Amish were more tolerant of members who joined the Mennonites. The founders of the Andy Weaver Amish disagreed, claiming that members should be shunned unless they confess and are accepted back into their Amish faith. The Andy Weaver Amish have allowed the slow-moving vehicle (SMV) signs for their buggies. However, they have held the line on adoption of a front windshield and rearview mirrors. The Andy Weaver Amish permit indoor bathrooms and linoleum floors, but not the window blinds.

The most progressive group is the **New Order Amish.** This group started when a group in Holmes County, Ohio, in 1960 claimed that it was possible for believers to know that they have been saved. They cite the Gospel of John (5:24): "...*He that heareth my word, and believeth on Him that sent me, hath everlasting life, and shall not come into condemnation; but is passed from death unto life.*" They refer to this as a spiritual awakening. Other Amish believe that this resembles too much the practices of various evangelical Protestant denominations. Today, the New Order Amish are distinctive from the other affiliations in their adoption of Sunday school and Wednesday evening youth meetings to study the Bible. They are more conservative in emphasizing high moral standards, in restricting alcohol and tobacco use, and in courtship practices, but more liberal in their selective adoption of modern technology and entrepreneurship. For example, buggies of New Order Amish are allowed to have the slow-moving vehicle symbols plus reflector tape, sliding doors, a windshield, windshield wipers, rubber tires on wheels, rearview mirrors, and headlamp and turning signal lights that operate from battery power. New Order Amish homes have linoleum floors, indoor plumbing, central heating, and bottled gas appliances. On the farm, a tractor for hauling and transporting things around the farm is permissible. In the shop and self-owned businesses, portable electric generators provide power for lights and various tools and machines.

In the adoption of technology, the Old Order Amish are not much different from the New Order Amish. The Old Order Amish are more restrictive on the use of electric lights in the shops, on tractors with rubber tires, and gas-powered freezers in the home. The buggies of Old Order Amish members do not include sliding doors, windshield wipers, or rubber tires.

Church Service

Church districts are organized so that it is a convenient buggy ride for all members to each other's houses. In most communities, both large and small, this means that members live within ten miles of each other.

Services begin at 8:30 or 9:00 in the morning and last through the fellowship meal at noon. The actual service is about $3^1/_2$ hours. People stay around to visit after the meal until it is time to go home to do the evening farm chores. Both adults and children attend the service. There is no Sunday school (except among the New Order Amish) nor special services for children. Everyone, parents and children, meet in the home. Many times there will be 150 to 200 people crowded into the house. Most homes have movable partitions specially designed to make room for the entire congregation. All congregations have a "church" wagon that

In each church district, the members donate money to buy the church wagon. The church wagon stores the benches and the hymnals and is delivered a few days before to the member's residence where the Sunday service will be held.

carries the benches and hymnals from one house to the other for church services.

The Amish follow a very traditional order of service that has not changed much over the years. Men and women are segregated during the service. They enter the house by different doors and they sit in separate sections. The meal afterwards is also segregated by gender. Children normally sit with their mothers. Here is an example of a typical Sunday service:

Arrival and fellowship

Silence in the worship area

Congregational singing (mostly from the *Ausbund*, the
traditional hymn book of the Amish)

Leaders meet in a separate room to discuss issues and agree
on the order of preaching and prayers for the service

Opening sermon

Silent kneeling prayer

Scripture reading by the deacon

Main sermon, which may last over an hour

Affirmations from ordained leaders and lay members

Kneeling prayer, which is a prayer read by the minister

Benediction, or blessing and encouragement

Closing hymn

Members meet occasionally to discuss specific issues

Meal (prepared by the women)

Fellowship during and after the meal

One little known fact about Amish church life is that church

The house is the location of Sunday service, and must accommodate 200 and more people. Church districts are relatively compact areas so that a buggy ride to a member's house is not too difficult.

leaders are chosen by **lot**. There is no formal training or other qualifications to become a deacon, minister, or bishop. This practice is based on several New Testament passages that emphasize the importance of honest men with good hearts, such as the following passage from Acts of the Apostles (1:24-26): *"And they prayed, and said, Thou, Lord, who knowest the hearts of all men, show of these two the one whom thou hast chosen, to take the place in this ministry and apostleship from which Judas fell away, that he might go to his own place. And they gave lots for them, and the lot fell upon Matthias and he was numbered with the eleven apostles."*

Both men and women members of the church district will nominate male members for office, but only if these men are considered role models living according to Amish faith and values. Usually, candidates must be nominated by at least two members. Nominees are asked to go into another room. *Ausbund* hymn books are placed on a table and a piece of paper with the biblical quote, such as the one above, is placed in one of the hymn books. The nominees walk back in and each one picks up a hymnal. The person who selects the hymnal with the paper is considered to have been chosen by God.

Communion and Council Meetings are on Saturday or Sunday and are held twice a year (during the fall and spring). Meetings of members within each church district are held in order to arrive at consensus on issues that could be dividing members. These new agreements become part of the *Ordnung*. Communion cannot proceed if there is serious disagreement on issues of importance to the members. A disagreement is a symbol of individuality, selfishness, and pride that goes against the way of living described earlier as *Gelassenheit.*

The communion service is longer than a regular service, normally beginning about 8:30 or 9:00 a.m. and lasting as long as eight hours. Morning worship can last three hours and covers the events in Genesis and Exodus. The afternoon service covers the life of Jesus in the New Testament. At the council meeting, members are exhorted to get themselves right with God and their neighbors. Many parts of the church districts' *Ordnung* are recited by the bishops, and the ministers ask each member for their agreement. If there are no serious disagreements, communion proceeds. The bishop breaks the bread and members pass around a cup of grape wine. The communion service concludes with the members washing each other's feet.

Confession can be either a private or public affair, depending upon the seriousness of the offense. With less serious violations of the *Ordnung*, the deacon and a minister visit the offender and ask for an act of contrition and a promise to cease the behavior. In cases where the offense is considered serious, or if the offender has repeated the behavior even after a previous confession, the confession must be made publicly during a Sunday service. The church leaders will consider the nature of the offense, and the offender is asked to defend his/her position in front of the congregation. The person is asked to leave, and the leaders and congregation discuss the situation and agree on a course of action. The person returns to the service and is asked to conform. A public confession to a less serious offense is called a *sitting* confession. A more serious offense requires a *kneeling* confession. Very serious offenses result in a six-week (approximately) ban or avoidance of social contact (or *Meidung*) with the individual. Offenders who will not confess or who have committed the most serious offenses of all, such as adultery, are excommunicated. Excommunicated members can rejoin, but it is very difficult. They must convince the leaders and members that they are truly repentant.

An important Amish religious event is **baptism**. Young men and women decide to be baptized in their late teens and early twenties. Baptism symbolizes that a young man or woman has made a commitment to live according to Amish religious beliefs and according to the *Ordnung* of the church district. To the Amish, baptism represents a voluntary surrender of one's individuality to that of one's church district. Thus, the standards used by individuals in determining what they will wear, technology they will use, and manner in which they will speak are those standards prescribed in a church district's *Ordnung*. At this point in their lives, many Amish teenagers have been through their period of "sowing wild oats." That was the time after the eighth grade when they had some freedom to socialize on their own and begin a period of courtship. Most Amish boys and some of the girls have been working. Many times, if the employer is Amish, the money earned by the young man or woman is turned over to the parents. However, if the son or daughter works for an "English" employer, that is less likely the case.

Sometimes the money is not spent in ways that Amish parents would prefer. Some Amish boys may purchase a car, and sometimes Amish teenagers may get into trouble with the police for consuming alcohol or for being rowdy. Parents also are concerned about the influence "English" teenagers might have on their youth.

Despite these worries, over 80 percent of Amish sons and daughters decide to be baptized and join the church. By then, they have some familiarity with the non-Amish world and have decided that it is not for them. They may already have decided on who they will marry, but they cannot marry within the Amish faith until they are baptized.

Baptism is usually in the fall and is followed by several months of instruction by the church leaders. The instructions review the history of the Amish, the basic tenets of the Amish faith, and the *Ordnung* of the church district. At the church service, the bishop asks the baptism candidates three questions, to which they must assent. The English translation of these questions is: *"Are you willing, by the help and grace of God, to renounce the world, the devil, and your own flesh and blood, and be obedient only to God and His church?; Are you willing to walk with Christ and His church and to remain faithful through life and until death?; and, Can you confess that Jesus Christ is the Son of God?"* Each baptism candidate replies in the affirmative. The deacon pours water into the cupped hands of the bishop who in turn lets the water drip onto the candidate's head. The bishop then shakes the candidate's hand and welcomes the candidate as a full member of the church.

The **marriage** ceremony is usually held in the late fall, although spring weddings are becoming more popular. These ceremonies are generally on Tuesday or Thursday, except for the New Order Amish which hold the services on Saturday. The Amish do not marry until they have been baptized and become church members. The reader should note that widows and widowers may remarry any time during the year, and preparations are much less elaborate.

Courtship between a young man and woman is not secretive, but engagements are kept secret. Intentions to marry are announced about a month or two before the wedding. Weddings are big social affairs and involve a great deal of preparation in the home of the bride, where the wedding party is held. The marriage ceremony itself is carried out by the bishop. The bishop asks the bride and groom the marriage vows. An English translation of these vows sounds similar to the vows in many other Christian denominations: *"Are you now willing to enter wedlock together as God in the beginning ordained and commanded? Are you confident that this, our sister (brother), is ordained of God to be your wedded wife (husband)? Do you also promise your wedded wife (husband), before the Lord and His church, that you will nevermore depart from her (him), but will care for her (him) and cherish her (him), if bodily sickness comes to her (him), or in any circumstances which a Christian (husband) wife is responsible to care for, until the dear God will again separate you from each other?"*

Parents of the bride and groom generally are not in attendance at the ceremony because they are too busy supervising the preparations for the wedding party. Unlike "English" weddings, the parents of the bride and groom are not accorded any special sta-

The gravestones in an Amish cemetery are not fancy, consistent with their beliefs.

tus. The wedding reception includes singing hymns, eating, and playing games. The bride and groom usually spend the first night at the house of the bride. The next several weeks involve the newly married couple visiting their families and friends.

In all societies, **funerals** symbolize an opportunity for the surviving family and friends to remember and pray for the deceased, and to find expressions for their own grief over the loss of the individual. For the Amish, it is preferable to die at home. By telephone, the news of a death is transmitted to those who need to know but live in other communities far away. Even on short notice, many Amish will travel in a group by train or a van driven by an "English" neighbor to attend a funeral service.

The deceased is dressed in white: men in a shirt, trousers, and socks; and women in a dress, cape, and cap. The coffin is usually made of wood and is simple in design. Some have linings, but some Amish groups do not permit this. Except among the most conservative groups, bodies are prepared for burial at a funeral home, and returned to the home until burial.

The funeral is normally held in the home of the deceased. There is a short sermon that talks about the person who died, and a longer sermon by a minister who is a guest from another church district who talks about the purpose of death. This is followed by a short eulogy and a period for mourners to view the deceased one last time. Men from the church district, but not close relatives, prepare the grave site. Generally, the Amish have their own cemeteries, although some Amish have plots in regular community cemeteries or those of Mennonite congregations nearby.

There is a procession to the graveyard and the pallbearers throw the dirt back onto the coffin. When the grave is about halfway full, a short hymn may be sung. After the burial, it is customary for everyone to gather at someone's house for a meal, a practice common with many religious groups. The meal is symbolic of life and helps those close to the deceased to begin a process of healing and to continue with their lives within the church district, and with their neighbors and their friends.

4

Amish
Community
Life

"The barn raising...
was large attended for this area;
close to 100 men, boys from surrounding areas...
It was a beautiful day and the barn was
almost complete by evening."

The Budget, May 1990

⌒Amish Community Life⌒

A frequently asked question when two strangers meet is: "Where are you from?" The answer given can conjure up a wide array of images. If an individual says, "I'm from Brooklyn in New York City," then the images are a lot different than if the individual replies, "I'm from Ames, Iowa." Life teaches us that people are different because of the kinds of communities in which they grew up, and in which they presently live. Their experiences are different, their politics are different, and their values, beliefs, and preferences are different. Although sometimes our images of places create false stereotypes about the individuals who live there, it remains true that our first impressions of strangers we meet are formed by finding out about where they live.

Most Americans have one thing in common: they are proud of where they live and although everyone complains about the things they would like to see improved in their communities, most become quite defensive when an outsider offers similar criticism. It is this identification with where one lives that defines what a community is all about. Communities are geographic places, to be sure, but they are much more. Communities are the places where people live their lives on a day-to-day basis, and they are the places from which people experience the rest of the world. Although people in the United States and Canada move frequently and travel often, it still remains a fact that most people live near their relatives, and most of their friends live nearby too. Without a doubt, for better or for worse, communities and the kinds of people who live there influence the quality of our lives.

Community is an extremely important aspect of Amish life because their religious values emphasize the importance of living together as a community of believers. In addition, they have learned the lessons of history. There are no more Amish left in Europe, in part because it was more difficult for them to own land, to live close together, and to worship together. In the United States and Canada, they could acquire enough land to form close-knit communities, where people could associate on a face-to-face basis, and live according to their religious beliefs.

Most tourists who visit Amish communities are from urban places, and are accustomed to thinking about a community as a physical location. The physical locations for Amish communities are called **settlements**. A settlement is a cluster of Amish families living near each other. Living closely together is important because it allows the Amish to come together for church services, to support schools for their children, and to help each other with farm and household chores. The *Ordnung* is mostly oral, and without face-to-face communication, the rules that govern the distinctive Amish way of life lose their relevance.

It is difficult to give an exact count of the number of communities, because new ones are forming all the time, and on occasions, some communities become extinct. However, today, there are over 350 Amish communities in the United States and Canada. About half of these communities were founded since 1990. Most of the settlements or communities are in the Midwestern states, but the location of settlements extends as far north as Lucknow in west central Ontario, Canada, as far south as Beeville, Texas, as far east as central Delaware, and as far west as the state of Montana.

Pennsylvania has the most communities with 48, followed by Ohio (42), Wisconsin (42), Michigan (34), Missouri (26), and Kentucky (24), New York (21), Indiana (19). Although there are more communities in Pennsylvania, the state with the largest number of Amish is Ohio.

The greater **Holmes County community** in northeastern Ohio is the largest of all. It includes five different counties (Coshocton, Holmes, Stark, Tuscarawas, and Wayne). Over 30,000 Amish (about one in every seven Amish) live there. The second largest and oldest is the **Lancaster County community** in southeastern Pennsylvania. It includes Amish from the neighboring counties of Chester and York. It is the most famous of all Amish areas and has a great many tourist facilities, although the Holmes County area is catching up. The Lancaster County Amish population is about 22,000. Other large communities include the northern Indiana counties of **Elkhart** and **LaGrange** and an area about 50 miles east of Cleveland, Ohio, in **Geauga County**.

These and other large communities attract tourists and it is from these communities that popularized images about the Amish are formed. The fact of the matter is that most Amish communities are small, containing only one or two church districts. However, nowadays, even areas where there are small communities see the

Amish Communities: 1950

Amish Communities: 2004

development of a few businesses that cater to tourists.

Most Amish communities are new. One little known fact is that only 19 Amish communities existed at the turn of the century. In fact, about two-thirds of the 220 plus settlements were started within the past 35 years. Why is this? The answers are simple: population growth and the search for more farmland.

During the nineteenth century, several Protestant denominations targeted the Amish for conversion, and in the 1860s, there was a large schism among the more traditional (now called the Old Order) and progressive Amish groups who over time became identified as Mennonites. By 1900, there were only about 5,000 Amish men, women, and children in the United States and Canada. Since 1900, as the history of the Amish tells us, the schisms have been internal between more conservative and more progressive Amish groups, but they are all still Amish. The Amish are very successful at raising their daughters and sons to accept the Amish faith. Four of every five Amish sons and daughters decide to be baptized Amish and live according to the Amish way of life.

Altogether, the Amish population is increasing rapidly and the search for new communities is a constant source of discussion among church elders and members alike. Where are the newer Amish settlements today? Ohio and Pennsylvania remain important states for the spread of Amish to new areas. Since 1990, 10 new communities have started in Pennsylvania, and 21 in Ohio. Other states include Wisconsin (24 new communities), New York (10), Michigan (13), Kentucky (14), and Missouri (15).

Comparing the total number of communities to the number that is new, the reader can see that the Amish presence in these five states is almost entirely from recent establishments.

Areas in these states are well suited for the Amish. They have large sections that have remained rural, yet are near urban centers that offer health facilities and other services that the Amish

Newer Amish settlements have concentrated in rural areas where the terrain is rolling, and agricultural land is still available.

require from time to time. These states have long traditions of family-based agriculture, with diversified farms that include both grain crops and livestock (especially dairy). The topography of many new Amish settlements is ideal for horse-farming (rolling hills). It is not easy to start a new community; and sometimes communities fail because they are unable to attract a sufficient number of families to maintain a church district, or because it is difficult to buy land, or due to the competition for land from real estate developers. One community in Ohio that has declined and is near extinction is about 25 miles northwest of Columbus. Only a few families are left in the area and the cost of land has become prohibitively high.

Common sense already tells us what anthropologists and sociologists have discovered through their research: that communities are more than physical places. They are locations where people live, work, raise their children, and go to church.

Amish communities are no different. Social scientists have found that communities play five important roles. The **first** is that communities have their **own economies**. Communities are places where products are made and services are available. Amish communities are distinctive for their local economies. Amish communities are rural and most are also agricultural. Less than 2 percent of all Americans today live on a farm. The percentage is many times higher for the Amish, although the proportion of Amish families who depend on agriculture varies from community to community. In the greater Holmes County community about 20 percent of Amish breadwinners are farmers. Amish communities are also distinctive for what they produce because beyond agriculture, other well-known products made by the Amish include furniture of all kinds, buggies, and leather products for horses.

In Amish communities, there still exists the traditional division of labor in the family. The husband is the breadwinner and the wife takes care of the house. This does not mean that women are not important to the economy. Growing a garden, canning food, and helping out on the farm are important economic roles for women. Some women do piecework, such as quilts, to bring in extra money and a few even own their own businesses. For example, some women have started restaurants in their homes or garages converted over for serving food. The good reputation of family style Amish cooking has created a big demand. Busloads of people have a chance to eat a lunch or dinner prepared by Amish women, and to more directly experience the Amish lifestyle than they could by going to one of the tourist restaurants. The tourist should be advised that most of these homes only serve groups who have scheduled in advance.

Compared to the average American worker, Amish husbands are more likely to be self-employed as farmers, blacksmiths, furniture makers, etc. Often the family business includes a brother, a son, a nephew, or other members of the extended family. In some Amish communities, especially the larger ones, many Amish husbands work for non-Amish employers, such as carpenters for a construction company or assemblers on a factory line. These businesses have relocated to Amish areas because of the Amish reputation for hard work and reliability.

The economy of Amish communities differs from "English" communities because of what they buy. Their restrictions on the use of technologies that depend on electricity creates a different lifestyle. Hardware stores in Amish areas display refrigerators, stoves, and lights that operate by propane or kerosene. Many blacksmiths are needed for the large number of horses (both work and buggy). Folk medicines and vitamin supplements are sold at the many bulk food stores.

Surrounding and permeating the larger Amish communities is the tourist trade. Restaurants, museums, quilt shops, bed and breakfast operations, and a plethora of other businesses cater to the tourist. Some tourist businesses are more authentically Amish than others, and a few tourist establishments are actually Amish owned. A few Amish may work for these businesses, but most Amish families do not rely on the tourist trade. In a way, what tourists see when they come to Amish country is two communities, one Amish and one non-Amish. The non-Amish community includes local people who, like the Amish, must put up with the tourist traffic, as well as the tourist businesses that are often owned by outsiders. This is especially true in the Lancaster County community area of Pennsylvania. In the greater Holmes County community, a larger share of the tourist businesses are locally owned. A visitor to both communities can probably notice the difference this makes in the "flavor" of the two areas.

A **second** role played by all communities is as a place to raise children, and as well, to reinforce among adults the values they learned early in life. This is called **socialization.** This is why in American society some families will move from what they believe to be the so-called negative influences of big cities to the positive influences of more rural communities.

A traveler in an Amish area will note the large number of children. They are walking on the side of the road to and from school, running an errand, or visiting with friends. They are helping their fathers in the field and their mothers with the home chores, or they are driving buggies (a very important reason to be careful when driving a car in Amish areas).

The tourist may notice the number of one-room schools in an Amish community. These parochial schools have been established by the Amish because of concerns about compulsory education through the twelfth grade, content of the curriculum taught in the public schools, and matters of discipline. However, most noticeable if one lives in an Amish community for an extended period of time, is the importance of learning values through the family (and the extended family). Amish value the face-to-face, personal communication that takes place in the family, among Amish neighbors, and with fellow members of the same church district. It is through the personal nature of the Amish way of life that Amish values are learned by children and reinforced among adults.

The **third** role played by all communities is enforcement of standards of behavior and values of importance to members. This is called **social control**. The phrase "social control" immediately conjures up the image of the police, but social control also is exercised by communities through zoning regulations, city/county ordinances, and local school policies. Most important of all, however, is that social control is not something forced on individuals by government, but is something that comes from within and from every member of the community. For example, in communities with low crime rates, neighbors are more likely to care about each other, to trust each other, to watch out for each other's property, and to call the police if they see something suspicious.

In Amish communities, social control means living within the boundaries or fence established by the *Ordnung*. Each baptized member of the church district participates in a continuing dialogue about what it means to be Amish and to live according to the *Ordnung*. In addition, the face-to-face, more personal nature of relationships among the Amish, their distinctive dress, and the way some "English" dress and behave, is a constant reminder to the Amish of who they are and what it means to be Amish.

The **fourth** role of a community is providing people opportunities to participate in social events, and to join various groups. This is called **social participation**. One feature that distinguishes American society and culture from the peoples of other countries is how much they value volunteering. In typical American

Pine Craft is both a permanent community of Amish and a popular vacation spot for Amish from the north. Most Amish visitors arrive by bus and are greeted by those already there.

communities, there are dozens and even hundreds of volunteer organizations, from the fire department, to civic groups, to local sports leagues. These organizations are at the center of a community's social life and the participation of members in the civic and social affairs of the places where they live.

Amish communities present opportunities for participation in social events. There are church services which are rotated from house to house of each member in a church district. These services are marked by extended visiting and food being served afterwards. Young people engage in "Sunday singings," which are opportunities for boys and girls to meet. Plus, there is a constant round of informal visiting and gossiping about local events. Many Amish, on occasion, go into town to eat at a restaurant. In the greater Holmes County community a couple of the local McDonald's have hitching posts, and one has a special sign instructing buggy drivers where to park. Amish will visit zoos and museums and other places where families can relax and enjoy a few hours away from work and school. Getting there requires them to hire a van, which is driven by a non-Amish person. These can often be seen on the roads in Amish areas. Many Amish vacation in a small community near Sarasota, Florida, called Pine Craft. Most Amish vacationers take buses to get there.

The **fifth** and final role played by communities is that of people helping each other out. This is called **mutual support**. To the tourist, the first thing that probably comes to mind is a "barn-raising." In fact, at the various tourist businesses in an Amish area, videos of barn-raisings have become big sellers. Certainly,

An important symbol of community for Americans is mutual support and volunteerism. Among the Amish, this is symbolized by the barn-raising.

a barn-raising is an important symbol of mutual support. When a farmer's barn burns down or is destroyed by a storm, the livelihood of the whole family is threatened. In all American communities, natural disasters and emergencies bring out the best in human nature. People eagerly pitch in and help rebuild. In this sense, the Amish and the "English" are alike. However, the Amish have maintained a deeper sense of mutual support that has been lost in many communities as American society evolved from an agrarian, rural base to today's predominately urban and suburban lifestyles. Although there are many excellent examples of American communities where people help each other every day, and without a great deal of fanfare, it remains true that mutual support among people declines as a society becomes modern and urban. In contrast, the Amish have been more successful in maintaining the value of helping each other on a daily basis, especially around the farm and home. It is difficult for the average tourist to see examples of mutual support through the windows of their passing cars, save for the occasional barn-raising, but it is there and it is real, and it helps define the Amish as a distinctive group of people who are living a lifestyle often envied by others.

5

Amish *Family* Life

"No culture has ever been able to provide
a better shipyard for building storm-proof vessels
for the journey of man
from the cradle to the grave
than the individual nourished in a loving family."

The Budget, July 1991

⌒Amish Family Life⌒

Family life is important in all societies. Some of the most important issues in American society today center on issues surrounding the family. The political parties compete with each other, claiming to be more supportive of the family than their opponents. The focus on the family in American society is not without justification. As American society became more urban, the nature of families changed. There are many more single-parent families, and blended families with children of both the husband and wife from previous marriages. In contrast to 30 years ago, both parents are likely to work and the amount of time parents and children spend together has decreased greatly.

These changes have caused Americans to be concerned about the future direction of the family, and therefore of the future welfare of society in general. Many people are curious about and attracted to the Amish because they have maintained the traditional family unit, and as well, the extended family of grandparents, aunts, uncles, and cousins remains important and viable.

Family life among the Amish is strong because family members feel a strong sense of belonging and because all members work as a team to keep the family functioning both economically and spiritually. There is a feeling of mutual obligation in loaning land, money, material goods, and assistance to other family members in times of need, and in addition, there is strong emotional support among family members.

Whatever the Amish do, they do in family units. Only 7 percent of the Amish households are single-person units, compared to about one-quarter of "English" homes. Almost all single-person households adjoin other Amish homes. The majority of Amish live in a household with six or more persons that often includes grandparents and other members of the extended family. Aunts, uncles, and cousins are likely to live across the road or on the farm next door. Many Amish homes have the *"dawdy haus"* which is right next to and even attached to the original structure. The *"dawdy haus"* is where elderly parents move when they "retire" and give the farm and larger house over to one of their children. It can hardly be considered a retirement, however, for the parents help their adult children's new families in whatever way they can.

In American society, influence can decline with age. Older people are often considered out of touch with new technologies and new knowledge. In Amish society, the elderly are considered important givers of advice about almost everything, including health and illness, household chores and cooking, gardening, farming, and predicting the weather. Boys frequently follow in the footsteps of their fathers, taking up the same job, and learning how to run the farm or business by helping their fathers, or by working for an uncle or grandfather. Girls learn from their mothers, aunts, and grandmothers, and, increasingly, girls too acquire business and trade skills by working alongside family members in a family-owned business.

The movement toward the equality of genders has had little influence on Amish families. Amish women believe that they are to submit to their husband's authority, but this does not mean they are without influence. They are responsible for raising their families, providing for the needs of the home, and assisting their husbands on the job. For example, in one family, the wife and daughters spend time cleaning the office and employee lunch area of a small Amish-owned manufacturing company. Many Amish women do the bookkeeping or record-keeping. Even with help from the children, it is difficult to manage a household of six to eight people. They supervise the canning, cooking, cleaning, washing, sewing, mending, gardening, and yard work.

In the church, women hold no formal authority. Women cannot be ordained as ministers, deacons, or bishops. However,

Religious values of the Amish place great importance on children. Raising children is the responsibility of both parents. As well, older brothers and sisters help with the younger ones.

they do participate in church meetings because they are baptized members. They also can nominate men for leadership positions.

Some outsiders have presumed that Amish women are oppressed. While Amish women are not liberated by "English" standards, their roles in the family and the church are clear. Husbands are busy running the farm or other business, and wives are busy running the household (and sometimes their own business, such as quilt-making). If "liberation" is having daily control over how one lives, then within the "fences" of Amish values, Amish women may be more liberated than many outsiders realize. Anyone who has ever worked for a large corporation or bureaucracy knows how unliberating the modern world of business can be.

Amish youth marry between the ages of 20 and 25. Marriage is highly esteemed and raising a family is like a professional career for Amish adults. Nine out of 10 adults are married, and widowers and widows are very likely to remarry. Marriage vows are rarely broken. In extreme cases, couples may live apart, but divorce is taboo. Divorced people are automatically excommunicated because it is a very serious violation of the *Ordnung*. Amish believe in large families. Birth control is usually not practiced until the fourth or fifth child is born, and then quietly, since it is officially forbidden. Over time Amish families have become smaller, but this has been a slow, steady change caused by the number of young husbands struggling to start their own business or working in factories, as farming has become less of an option. The opportunity to value children as helpers on the farm has diminished, but children can still share in the upkeep of the house and help the father if he runs his own business. Many young Amish men find part or full-time work for an Amish employer, and many of the girls will work in restaurants and other tourist businesses. The money they earn is contributed back into the family or put away so that later on the money can be used to buy a farm or start a business. Too much spending money only becomes a temptation. Even with the transition out of farming, children are still considered a blessing and remain highly valued among all Amish.

Daily life is spent in the context of the family. Children may be born at home, although less so than in the past. In the greater Holmes County community, there is a special birthing center located in the small town of Mt. Eaton. It was developed specifically as a place for Amish women, but serves the local Mennonite population as well. It is staffed by nurses, and directed by a physician.

The daily life of the Amish is centered around the home. Children play at home, and school is within easy walking distance. By age fourteen, children are working full-time at home or nearby in the shop or family business. Recreational activities take place at home or with nearby neighbors. Young couples are married at home. Church services rotate from home to home. Most meals are eaten at home. Social gatherings, such as quiltings, singings, and frolics are held at home. Hair is cut at home. The women make most of the clothes that the family wears.

Amish families are tied to a geographic area much more than contemporary American families. Many Amish live within several miles of their childhood homes. Geography and family are tied together, and roots to both are strong. A typical Amish child may have many uncles and aunts living in the area, plus dozens of cousins.

Mealtime is a time for the whole family to come together. Everyone sits down at the same time and remains at the table until all have finished eating. The children take their places on benches along the side of a long table, resembling a picnic table. The parents sit on chairs at each end of the table. The father asks for silent prayer before the meal begins. Serving dishes are passed and the meal proceeds with a minimal amount of talking, except for polite conversation when guests are present. At the end of the meal, the father asks for a silent prayer again. Afterwards, there is often a Bible lesson, unless there are urgent outside chores to be finished, or when the older children may be leaving for a youth gathering.

Each child has assigned chores to complete before school, and in the evening upon their return. In the summer the children weed the garden and mow the lawn in the evening. Of course, if the Amish family has cows, they must be milked early in the morning (usually before breakfast) and again in the evening. The lunch pails need to be washed and packed for the next day. There is no food service at Amish schools, and the men and older boys who work away from home will need to pack their lunch as well. This could mean the daily preparation of 6 lunches or more in a typical Amish home.

When all the chores are completed, the family members may gather to play games. The parents often participate in playing softball, volleyball, and board games with the children. The Amish do not have radios, TVs', and computers, so they spend more time interacting with each other. Often, birthdays are celebrated with cake or cupcakes. When asked, one teenager said it was good to belong to a large family because it made the chores go faster, and there was always someone to play with.

The transition of Amish out of farming into self-owned businesses and factory work is of concern because it affects the family more than any other aspect of Amish life. This shift is often referred to as the "lunch pail" threat by church leaders. The symbol of the Amish husband taking a lunch box or pail to work means that he is leaving the home to go somewhere else in order to make a living. It becomes more difficult in this situation for sons to work alongside their fathers and learn both farming and the Amish way of life. In addition, the husband becomes subject to a less flexible time schedule, and it becomes more difficult to take off in order to attend weddings, funerals, barn raisings, and other traditionally important events in Amish society.

Weddings are a time of great excitement and are often planned a year in advance. The wedding service is held in the home or a shed which has been constructed to accommodate the wedding and for church services. The ceremony starts at 8:30 a.m. The men and young boys sit on one side and the women sit on the opposite side, each facing toward the center. The wedding party sits in between the two groups facing each other. "English" friends arrive later, after the service has started, and are seated together.

The bride usually selects a shade of blue for her dress and her two attendants wear identical dresses and aprons. Likewise, the groom's two attendants are dressed like the groom with dark trousers, a vest, and a white shirt.

Several deacons, preachers, and a bishop will preside over the service, preaching and praying in high German. The mothers of the bride and groom usually do not come to the service until it is about time to take the vows, as they are busy preparing the food. The ceremony continues until noon.

Many Amish families rent the "wedding" wagon. This is a service provided by their "English" neighbors. The wagon holds the tablecloths, silverware, glasses, cups, and any other table service needed for a large wedding of 300 to 500 and more people. It also carries large pots, bowls, serving dishes, and tables to prepare the meals. In the past, the family would borrow these things from neighbors and relatives, but times have changed.

The "wedding" wagon service is about $1.00 per place setting. The dishes, pots, and bowls are washed and placed back in the wagon. Of course, there is no dishwasher at an Amish home, except for the women who help, so all this washing is done by hand.

The availability of the "wagon" may determine when the wedding can be held. Thursday and Tuesday are the preferred days. However, with more Amish men working off the farm, they have begun to plan weddings for Saturdays. Weddings used to be held in the fall, after the harvest. Again, preferences for wedding dates changed as the economics of the Amish changed. Today, like other Americans, May and June are popular times for weddings amongst the Amish.

Wedding invitations are sometimes engraved, sometimes handwritten, and sometimes the invitation is merely verbal. It is an honor to be asked by the bride's family to be a server. Servers are the friends and cousins of the bride and groom. Depending on the number of people invited, the servers may be 30 or 40 in number to accommodate all the wedding guests. Sometimes the number of guests is so large that the tables must be cleared and reset for the next shift of guests.

The wedding meal consists of chicken, mashed potatoes, dressing, gravy, mixed vegetables, tossed salad, iced tea, water, coffee, cake, strawberry pie, and ice cream. Food is served "family" style and continuously passed around until everyone is full.

Before the meal begins, a prayer is sung, plus, there is a silent prayer. After eating, "English" friends usually go to the table with the wedding party to wish the bride and groom well. Most "English" friends leave early, and the remaining Amish begin to sing.

The bride and groom will usually stay overnight in a home they have prepared and return the next day to help clean up after the wedding party. They will take a trip later.

The authors asked an Amish woman to keep a diary of family activities for two midwinter days. Here is her record:

"**Sunday, December 31:** Hi, my name is Miriam. Brr!!! Cold winter morn. I overslept. I run for the barn fearing I'm late for my morning job of doing the milkers, but thankfully I'm not, so I don't say how long I slept, and quickly do them.

"Back to the house and I put breakfast on. We have Bible reading and breakfast. 7:15 a.m.—time for the children to get up if we want to be in church on time. If we start a bit earlier getting ourselves ready Sunday morning, we save a lot of the rush! Brent says he's too sick to go, but we doctor him up and all go. There's been a lot of flu around. Services begin at 9:00 a.m. and usually last till noon, then we eat the noon meal at church which consists of bread, cold meat, cheese, pickles, jam, coffee, and cookies.

"We come home at 2:30 p.m., rest and read, then hot vegetable soup for supper at 4:30 before milking. After chores, Jeff and Josiah go to the young folks' singing. Afterwards they're invited to a friend's home and they play games and eat, etc., till late! It's New Year's Eve morn so I guess they'll plan to rest then. We spend the evening at home. On cold winter evenings when your way of transportation is horse and buggy, then your evenings are usually spent at home. But then that's when I love to be home.

"P.S. We did run over to Grandma's house though in the evening and had our fill of good roasted nuts and steaming hot coffee!

"**January 1:** I was awake early to soak up the peace and solitude that only a mother can appreciate before her brood awakens. 4:30 a.m.—hubby and 16-year-old Josiah went to chore and milk 30 Holsteins. I went to the basement and did all the laundry early in the morning. Afterwards I went to the barn to wash the milkers and clean up the milk house. Also made my daily routine to the pig barn—a new litter of baby pigs greeted me. I do the teeth pinching and give shots, etc. with the new litter.

"7:00 a.m.—Breakfast time. Our family, which consists of John and I, 19-year-old Jeff, 16-year-old Josiah, 12-year-old Krista, 8-year-old Brent, and 3-year-old Monica, usually eats together in the morning. Jeffrey has a job with a plumbing business—being it's New Year's he's got off of work today, also, no school today. Usually Krista and Brent go to school and Monica keeps us busy at home. She's a fun girl too. So Krista and I clean up the house, and stir together two big batches of cookie dough. Mom invites us to her house for pork and sauerkraut at noontime! What a treat for our family—also a great cooking break for me. I make a kettle of mashed potatoes to take along. She lives close by on the farm.

"After dinner I read and rest a bit—I'm getting Monica settled down for her p.m. nap. Then I tackle the chilled cookie dough. I bake lots of chocolate chip oatmeal cookies. We've planned to visit a neighbor and friends that will soon be leaving for Florida this p.m. So at 3 p.m. I pack up and take several of my fresh cookies, go find John—to see if he's ready to go. He says not yet. He's changing oil in the chicken house diesel, and getting things ready for the flock of 20,000 birds to go tonight. So I wait a while, then we go. It's getting to be milking time soon, but both our older sons are here tonight, and they will start milking. It's very nice with children this age. Probably this is the nicest time we'll have, the children all at home yet but at an age where we can all help on the farm. We have 160 acre farm—my home place.

"After chores I make coney sauce sandwiches, leftover dessert that we'd had for dinner, as our supper.

"Our winter evenings are usually games, reading, hot chocolate or coffee—whatever we wish. A time of family togetherness. We are blessed indeed. After family prayer, everyone is off to bed. Good night."

6

Amish
Education

"Tuesday…many gathered at the Miller's
to quilt the schoolteacher's quilt
with all her pupils' names on that she taught…
They gave her the quilt Friday
at the school picnic."

The Budget, June 1991

⌁Amish Education⌁

At the turn of the century, most Americans went to schools that were similar to Amish schools today. Schools were one-room structures, and many had outside plumbing. Organized sports were not very important. The vast share of students attended school only through the elementary grades, and most never graduated from high school. Many students stayed home to help during planting and harvesting seasons. The older students helped the younger students, and the one teacher taught all of the subjects to all of the students and at all grade levels. The subjects taught were the traditional three Rs of reading, (w)riting, and (a)rithmetic.

As American society changed, so too did American schools. There are few one-room schools left today. Most schools have

Amish schools are easy to see from the road. They are small, usually with one classroom, and have swings and a softball field.

long since consolidated and range in size from 500 to 5,000 students. Students attend school through the twelfth grade. Teachers are now subject matter specialists. All in all, a student from the early 1900s would find only a little to recognize in the school of the late 1990s.

As schools in the greater society changed, the Amish began to develop their own parochial school system. Today, most Amish children attend Amish parochial schools, where the teacher is Amish and so are all of the children. The school is sponsored by one or more of the church districts, and the board members are all Amish. Parents are closely involved in the affairs of the school, and the upkeep of the school building (including its construction) is accomplished through the volunteer labor of these same parents.

Formal Learning

The Amish formal education system includes grades one through eight, taught by one (sometimes two) teacher in a one-room school with an enrollment of 25 to 50 students. The majority of Amish children attend parochial schools. Some attend public schools, but often the majority of the students in the local public school are Amish too.

The Amish used to send their children to public schools; however, the movement toward consolidation of rural schools, and compulsory education, caused the Amish to reconsider their participation in public schools. Their main concern was that these changes would expose their children to values not consistent with an Amish way of life—too much individualism, too much academic and athletic competition, and too much secularism.

The first Amish parochial school was started in 1925; however, the parochial school movement did not really take hold and expand until after World War II. In 1960, there were 82 schools in seven states. Today, there are well over a thousand parochial schools, with a total enrollment of 30,000 plus "scholars," the name given to Amish students.

The one-room school is similar to that of the public one-room schools found throughout the rural United States in the early 1890s. The floor plan for a one-room Amish school is simple and straightforward. Desks are arranged in columns and face the teacher's desk. Behind the desk is the blackboard. A wood or coal stove serves as the primary source of heat, and kerosene lamps provide illumination. The school has no electricity or running water. Outside toilets, marked "boys" and "girls," are located toward the edge of the school yard. The school yard is used for recess on days when the weather is good. Often, there is a ball diamond so that the young people can play softball. However, in both games and sports, cooperation is emphasized, and competition is discouraged.

The school year begins about September 1 and continues until the end of April. School is held Monday through Friday, and there are few vacation days, with the exception of Thanksgiving and Christmas.

The day begins around 8:00 a.m. and concludes about 2:30 p.m. A typical schedule includes these activities:

SUBJECT	GRADES	APPROXIMATE TIME
Arrival and Order	1-8	8:00-8:10
Reading	1-4	8:10-9:00
Arithmetic	5-8	9:00-9:30
Recess	1-8	9:30-9:45
Arithmetic	1-4	9:45-10:30
Reading	5-8	10:30-11:30
Lunch and Recess	1-8	11:30-12:15
English	1-8	12:15-1:30
Recess	1-8	1:30-1:45
Spelling	1-8	1:45-2:30

Dismissal

The curriculum consists of reading, spelling, phonics, vocabulary, English, geography, arithmetic, penmanship, and Bible lessons. In addition, both English and German are required subjects. English is required by law and is the language that connects the Amish to the greater society, especially for business and professional services. German, however, is the language that provides continuity with the past and reinforces their identity as Amish.

Most teachers are Amish women who have not yet married. Most are in their mid twenties. There is no certification requirement for being a teacher in an Amish school. The school board, composed of parents, picks the teacher they think will best serve as an example of the Amish way of life. The character of the teacher is of utmost importance to parents, school board members, and church leaders alike.

Teacher training is mostly informal, and primarily involves

self-directed learning. Many teachers help in schools for several years before they assume full-time duties. This serves as their apprenticeship. Summer months are used by Amish teachers for study and review of subjects. Annual regional and state meetings of Amish teachers provide an organized forum for the exchange of information about teaching, discipline, school policies, and other related matters. There is also a teachers' journal called the *Blackboard Bulletin*, which provides advice on all aspects of teaching, and is another way for teachers to exchange useful advice.

The most important subject is reading because it is fundamental to learning other subjects and is essential for getting along in

Amish schools group all 8 grades together in one room. Older students tutor the younger students.

life. Amish teachers believe that the most difficult part of their job is discipline, a concern they share with "English" teachers.

Published guidelines for Amish schools illustrate their view of education:

With the exception of devotion, it is the Amish theory
that the Bible be taught in the home and church; however,
it is further our aim to teach religion all day long in our
curriculum (lessons) and on the play-ground.
In Arithmetic by accuracy (no cheating).
In English by learning to say what we mean.
In History by humanity (kindness-mercy).
In Health by teaching cleanliness and thriftiness.
In Geography by learning to make an honest living from
the soil.
In Music by singing praises to God.
On the school ground by teaching honesty, respect, sincerity,
humbleness, and yes, the golden rule.

Amish parents are very involved in their schools. First, each family pays an annual tuition fee of around $1,000-1,500, regardless of the number of children who attend the school. Families with more resources will voluntarily increase their support. Second, parents may visit the school at any time, although they usually come to school for special programs at the end of the year and for their child's birthday. Most parents will visit the school several times during the school year. Third, although the church maintains the building, many of the parents help clean the school in preparation for the new school year. It is the children's responsibility to clean the school on a weekly basis. Finally, families will donate firewood and other essentials to the school.

Amish parents have continually refused to send their children to high school in the belief that additional education and contacts with non-Amish young people will only serve to encourage their youth to think and behave in nontraditional ways that are inconsistent with Amish values. Their resistance to compulsory education has brought them into conflict with school authorities in several states. The landmark Supreme Court case of *Wisconsin versus Yoder* of 1972 exempted the Amish from compulsory education laws. The Supreme Court recognized that education could continue outside the classroom, and that the *"enforcement of the State's requirement of compulsory formal education after the eighth grade would gravely endanger, if not destroy, the free exercise of (Amish) religious beliefs."*

Many readers may wonder how well Amish children perform on standardized tests. Past studies—using the Iowa Tests of Basics Skills in the areas of vocabulary, reading comprehension, word usage, knowledge, use of reference materials, and arithmetic problem solving—have found that the scores of Amish and non-Amish children were about the same. Additional comparisons using other national tests have reached the same conclusion. Despite clear differences in their approach to education, the quality of education training in Amish schools compares favorably with non-Amish schools.

Vocational Education

The world is changing and so have the Amish. As more and more Amish become involved in non-farm jobs, either in factories or as small business owners, special educational classes beyond the eighth grade become increasingly important. The

Amish also attend some technical training workshops and seminars to upgrade their skills in agriculture. Various county extension service offices in Amish areas conduct workshops which are customized for the needs of Amish farmers. These workshops cover topics such as improving milk production, improving feed rations, the use of no-till methods of planting and cultivation, the proper use of herbicides and pesticides, EPA regulations, swine production, and crop rotation. Amish sawmill operators in Ohio have attended lumber grading workshops sponsored by The Ohio State University's Agricultural Technical Institute at the Wooster campus in Wayne County.

Many Amish have been attending buggy safety programs sponsored by the Department of Food, Agricultural, and Biological Engineering at The Ohio State University. The Department is also working with Amish buggy makers to improve the safety and visibility of buggies. Many of the Amish schools have adopted buggy safety courses for their students.

Other special education seminars are also offered. For example, one local county health organization in Ohio conducted a special workshop for Amish church leaders on counseling in an effort to work more effectively with their church members. There are also special courses to explain Occupational Safety and Health Agency regulations to Amish business owners.

Informal Learning

It would be a misnomer to suggest that Amish education is simply "book learning." There is an informal system of education based on learning by seeing and doing what adults are doing. Girls learn about housekeeping, child rearing, gardening, and proper behavior in church and in relationships with others. So, too, boys learn proper behavior in church and with others, and learn about farming or the family business. In this informal system of education, the primary teachers are parents, grandparents, uncles, aunts, older brothers and sisters, members of the local church district, and Amish neighbors.

This network of extended family and fellow Amish provides a rich educational environment which contributes to the success of the Amish in raising their children to value the Amish faith. However, it should be kept in mind that alongside an environment conducive to learning how to be Amish is another environment, that of the world of the "English." Amish girls and boys know a lot about American life simply from the fact that it is all around them. Sometimes learning about two different ways of living can create an internal conflict. Amish families give their children, especially the boys, room to "sow their wild oats" during their adolescent years. Mostly this involves relatively minor acts of rebellion when compared to "English" teenagers. For example, a boy may own a car, but must be very discreet about where he parks it. Sometimes there is a problem with underage drinking. Naturally, Amish parents and church leaders are concerned about the behavior of their young people, but have faith that eventually young Amish men and women will make the decision to be baptized into the Amish faith.

Some non-Amish view this period of "sowing one's wild oats"

with too much alarm, and incorrectly declare that the influence of modern life will soon destroy the Amish. Anyone who knows even a little about the history of the Amish knows that they have long survived, and even thrived, despite pressures from the outside.

Many "English" regard the "rowdyism" of Amish teenagers as "hypocritical." Two things must be remembered. First, both Amish and "English" parents must put up with at least a little rebellion from their children, especially during adolescence. Yet, most parents maintain faith in their children and continue to help them grow into productive adults who lead a good life. Like all "English" parents, Amish moms and dads find these accusations of hypocrisy to be too judgmental. Second, in most Amish settlements, the proportion of boys and girls who decide to be baptized into the Amish faith and dedicate themselves to the Amish way of life is 80 percent, and even higher. Those who decide not to become Amish often join more progressive Mennonite denominations. Almost all Amish children, including those who "drop out," lead a Christian-based life of faith in God.

7

Amish

Economic

Life

"Today we had a real nice and much needed rain after
a dry spell. Men are busy thrashing wheat.
Some people are cutting oats…
First cutting of hay was a good crop but
second cutting looks more poor…
There are two farmers' markets going now up here
so a lot of baked goods are being made to sell
every week plus garden vegetables being sold…
The log home erections and building has slowed down,
the next project that is being worked on is erecting
a big house with 18 doors."

Excerpts from several reports in *The Budget*,
July and September 1991

⌒Amish Economic Life⌒

To most people, the words farming and Amish go hand in hand. To be sure, farming has been the primary way for the Amish to make a living, and farming is still the preferred way for most. However, since the 1960s, the number of Amish who farm has not kept up with the growth of the Amish population. There are more young Amish men who want to farm than there are farms available for them. In some communities, the number of Amish breadwinners who farm has declined. This decline has been most notable in the largest Amish communities, such as the greater Holmes County community in Ohio, the Lancaster County community area in Pennsylvania, the Elkhart–LaGrange County community area in Indiana, and the Geauga County community area in Ohio. In three of these largest of all Amish communities, directories which list membership of Amish families, also include the occupation of the husband (the Lancaster County Amish directory does not list occupations). In the most recent directory, the proportion of males who farm in the greater Holmes County community was about 20 percent. In Elkhart–LaGrange (the 3rd largest community), it was 28 percent, and in Geauga County (the 4th largest community), only 10 percent were farmers. As recently as 35 years ago, in these three communities, over two in every three Amish breadwinners were farmers.

Many of the smaller and newer communities have experienced the same thing. In one community of about 75 families in southern Ohio, despite the availability of land, only three families are supported by agriculture. The rest earn their living from working in sawmills, several of which are owned and managed by other Amish.

Meanwhile, the number of Amish men working in non-farm occupations has grown dramatically. For example, in the greater Holmes County community, the number of men working in non-farm jobs was about 300 in 1965. Now, the number of men working in factories and running their own businesses has jumped to nearly 6,000.

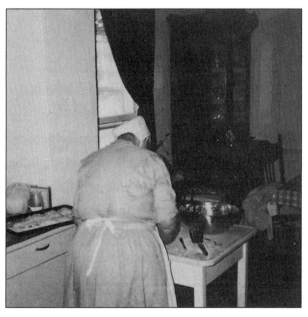

Amish women as homemakers play an important economic role in the family. Their skills in shopping, clothes-making, canning and preserving, gardening, and food preparation are vital to economic survival.

Despite this recent change, farming remains at the core of Amish values and way of life. It is their heritage and most Amish adults, including the men who work in non-farm jobs, grew up on a farm. Agriculture continues to be a symbol of separation from a world that has industrialized and urbanized, and will remain an important symbol as this century comes to a close.

Home Economics

Amish lifestyles are more austere and frugal than a typical American family. There are no bills to pay to the cable TV company and to public utilities for gas and electricity. Grocery bills are lower per person and little is spent on entertainment. Many clothes are made at home by the wife. She also provides a valuable economic service by raising a garden, canning hundreds of quarts of vegetables and fruits, and making many other things that most "English" have taken for granted can be bought at stores. Amish wives have also learned to make ends meet when shopping. Some foods are bought in bulk, and some Amish rent freezer space at a store or in the home of an "English" neighbor.

An Amish farm wife shared the household and farm budget with the authors. This family of 6 (husband, wife, and 4 children) receives its basic income from selling milk from a dairy herd of 33 Holstein cows. The farm has 160 acres, where they grow most of the hay, corn, and other grains needed to feed the cows. Their gross income last year was about $78,000. Half of this income goes to pay for farm expenses which include feeding and caring for the cows, growing crops, and paying the interest on the farm loan and various taxes, such as income and property tax.

The family budget for a typical month includes $150 for food, and $120 for fabric for the clothes the mother makes. Hardware supplies and repairs to lamps and lanterns, lawn mowers, and the washing machine costs another $125. Shampoo, soap, and personal hygiene items comes to about $25. Travel by bus and van (in an Amish taxi) is about $50. Another $55 is spent on cards, stamps, gifts, and miscellaneous items. Fuel costs add up to about $250 each month, for such things as propane, kerosene, and gas that run the lamps, lanterns, and refrigerators and milk cooler. There is a $280 per month payment for hospital and medical costs, as the Amish are self-insured. There was $30 for pizza for family and friends who helped with farm work. Finally, there was a one-time payment of $500, for fire insurance, or about $42 per month. (The Amish have their own fire insurance, too.)

This Amish family travels frequently, eats out regularly, subscribes to magazines and newspapers, and buys books. There are other costs as well that are more long-term, such as house maintenance, buggy maintenance, new furniture, and appliances and utensils for kitchen use. This family has a telephone for the farm and the monthly cost is about $25. Altogether, total monthly household expenses amount to about $1,600, or $20,000 per year.

The wife of the household manages the broiler operation for the family which brings in extra income (many Amish farms have contract broiler operations with poultry companies). She raises the broilers from one-day-old chicks until they are 6 to 7 weeks old, at which time they weigh about 5 pounds. The poultry processing company provides her with the chicks, the feed and medicines, and the market for the broilers.

The broiler house is 400 feet long and will hold 20,000 broilers at one time. The cost of the house was $150,000 and is amortized over a seven-year time period. The cost includes the brooders for the chicks, feeders and watering, and a diesel power unit instead of electricity for the operation.

This family receives about $5000 per batch of 20,000 broilers raised to 5 pounds in 6-7 weeks. This covers their costs and fuel for heating and the power unit. They estimate the annual gross income from this broiler project at about $35,000.

Farming

Tourists expect the Amish to be involved in farming, and think it special when from their passing autos they see Amish working in the fields. The Amish were farmers in Europe, and they readily took up farming when they moved to North America. Land was plentiful and fertile. Through the 1800s and the early years of the 20th century, the Amish way of farming did not differ very much from the way everyone else farmed. Farms were small and diversified, producing a wide variety of products, such as corn, wheat, hay, milk cows, pigs, chickens, and horses. Most of what they needed for their daily needs was provided by the farm. Surplus milk, vegetables, and fruits as well as baked goods were sold at the marketplace in order to earn money for staples at the store and to pay taxes.

Most Amish breadwinners today work in non-farm jobs, such as carpentry, even though the history and heritage of the Amish remains agriculture.

Farming in America began to change in the early 1900s with the introduction of motorized equipment, such as tractors, threshers, cultivators, and harvesters. In addition, chemical fertilizers, herbicides and pesticides, improved varieties of seeds and animals, and other agricultural advances changed the face of farming in America. Agriculture began a major shift from general farming to more specialized farming, which required increased investment in land, buildings, equipment, and more sophisticated management systems. Although the proportion of Amish men who are farmers has declined, the numbers are even lower for the rest of American society. The latest Census figures indicate that less than 1.5 percent of Americans live on a farm today.

While non-Amish agriculture developed into larger, more specialized farms, Amish farms remained small and diversified, relying on horses instead of tractors. This growing divergence in styles of farming has continued through the remainder of this century, although it would be a mistake for the reader to think that Amish farmers have not been innovative. The Amish farm of the late 21th century is in many ways different from the Amish farm of the 19th century. Amish farmers use some commercial fertilizer and other farm chemicals. Motors mounted or attached to wagons help power the machinery that threshes, cultivates, and harvests crops. Amish farmers use the same veterinary services as non-Amish farmers, and benefit from improved breeds of livestock and crop seeds.

Historically, farming for the Amish has been both a way to earn a living and a way to maintain their religiously based lifestyle. The Genesis passage in which God told Adam *"to till the ground from which he came"* provides a religious mandate for farming.

Machinery, such as these sit-down plows, are appropriate for horse-farming.

The Amish see themselves as caretakers of God's garden. The Amish believe they are to cultivate it carefully because it is their sustenance.

Amish farms vary in size from 80 to 150 acres. The number of acres is determined by how much land one man with a team of horses can plow, plant, and harvest. Crops usually follow a four-year rotation of corn, oats, wheat, and hay. Income from milk provides a regular paycheck which the farmer uses to farm operations and to maintain the home and family. Most field work is done by hand and with horsepower. For most Amish groups, no tractors are permitted for field work. Some of the more progressive Amish groups will use tractors around the barn to pull wagons and provide for belt power, but not to plow, disk, plant, cultivate, and harvest in the fields.

The use of horses for field operations helps to keep Amish farm size small enough for one man and his family to manage. It also keeps the pace of life slower (i.e., *Gelassenheit*), which is another advantage. Smaller size means that members of the Amish faith can live close enough to each other to permit face-to-face interaction, which, as we have mentioned, is important for the Amish way of life.

Since there is no electricity in either the house or the barn, gas lanterns are used for light. Especially during the winter months, barn chores are done without sunlight, so some form of artificial illumination is needed. Some Amish groups permit the use of milking machines while the more conservative groups still prohibit them. For those farmers who milk by hand, the customary number of cows for milking is between 10 and 15. For those who use a milking machine, the number is larger, usually about 20 to 35. Milking machines are run from a vacuum pump which is powered by a diesel engine. The bulk milk tank which keeps the milk cool (required by state regulations) is also powered by a diesel engine.

Amish farmers have adapted some modern hay making equipment to be pulled by horses. For example, they have mounted stationary gasoline engines on modern hay balers, which are then pulled by horses. Some Amish farm equipment manufacturers are building a special two-wheeled cart with a stationary engine which can be pulled by horses. This cart has sufficient power and attachments for farmers to use in a variety of tasks, such as cutting and binding hay. Harvesting wheat and oats is still done with the old-type binder. The binder cuts and bundles the grain and then ties it into sheaves. The farmer then stacks the sheaves into piles called shocks. The grain is allowed to dry before being hauled in wagons to the barn where threshing machines separate the grain and straw.

Corn is also harvested in bundles called shocks. Corn shocks in the field during the fall months presents a nostalgic view for tourists driving the roads in Amish communities. It gives them the impression that Amish farming is "old-fashioned." Although this may be partly true, the important point is that corn shocks have an important function in the small-scale farming style of the Amish. Some shocks are hauled to the barn where they are cut into small pieces and stored in the silo as silage. Silage is a high-protein feed used to increase milk production during the winter months when there is no fresh pasture for cows.

There is a clear division of labor in the Amish farm family. Husbands and sons do the field work, and gardening is the responsibility of women and small children. However, women will help during times of planting and harvesting when more hands are needed in the field to get the job done. Each farm has a garden. So do almost all of the homes of Amish families whose breadwinners do not make a living from agriculture. The women take charge of the planting, harvesting, and processing of the vegetables and fruits.

Today, nearly all farmers, Amish and "English," look for additional income-producing projects. For the Amish, one large conspicuous project has been the contract raising of broilers for sale to commercial markets. Large broiler processing operations

Raising broilers or chickens is one way Amish agriculture has diversified.

have contracted with individual farmers for the care and feeding of thousands of chickens for meat. The farmer provides a special building, usually about 400-500 feet long and about 40 feet wide, along with the equipment for feeding and watering the chickens. The farmer also provides the day-to-day care and management of the operation. The broiler company brings one-day-old chicks to the farm, and seven to eight weeks later comes back with large trucks to haul away the mature chickens for processing. Amish farmers are using modern scientific management to grow five- to six-pound live chickens, called broilers, ready for processing in less than two months. Each long poultry house can hold about 20,000 broilers. A contract farmer will go through the cycle of raising chickens 5 or 6 times every year. They are paid on a per-bird basis as well as a bonus for how much weight the chickens gain. It is estimated that they receive about 20 cents per bird for their work. This would produce about $5,000 per batch of 20,000 broilers. Out of this amount comes the cost for heat, the fuel for running the diesel engines that open the windows for ventilation and lift, drop the feeders, and keep a fresh water supply, and other miscellaneous costs.

The family farm usually is passed on to the youngest child. This may be different from the expectations of tourists, who might have assumed that the oldest child inherits the farm. However, the practice of the youngest boy taking over is a pattern of inheritance practiced in many of the German-speaking areas of Europe. In addition, it allows the Amish father to have gainful employment for a longer time before he retires.

The child who inherits the farm is expected to provide a place for his or her parents to live. This is called the grandparent or "dawdy haus," and is attached to or next to the main house. The income the parents receive from the sale of the farm is the money they use in retirement. Retirement is not a time of idleness. Grandparents also help out on the farm and with the grandchildren, and as well, grow their own garden to supplement the food they buy at the store.

Beyond Agriculture

The proportion of Amish who work in non-farm operations increases each year. The Amish provide a wide range of services through their non-farm businesses. They have four major sets of customers: other Amish; their "English" neighbors; "English" customers in more distant places who prefer the Amish because of their reputation for quality service; and of course, tourists.

There are four types of Amish micro-enterprises. The first type of Amish business is the **small cottage industry**. These are based at the residence, but are usually housed in a separate building dedicated to the operation of the business. These cottage industries are quite diverse and include bakeries, bicycle shops, bulk food stores, bookstores, cabinet shops, engine repair shops, greenhouses, harness shops, buggy repair shops, tool sharpening services, tarp shops, upholstery repair services, watch and clock repair, and quilt shops. Almost all of these businesses have fewer than five employees, and most of the labor is provided by family members.

Hundreds of non-farm Amish businesses dot the rural landscape today.

It is in the small cottage industries that some compromising has occurred in regard to the ownership and use of a telephone. A phone may be allowed in the shop, or in a telephone shanty nearby the shop. Its use is restricted to business purposes, although talking to regular customers by phone is always a time to catch up on news and gossip, as it is with "English" business people.

Second, there are **manufacturing and service businesses** that are owned and operated by the Amish. These include farm equipment manufacturing, bakeries, pallet shops, sawmills, buggy-making, production of parts for buggies, furniture-making, printing/publishing, repair shops, and an endless array of other enterprises. These businesses are larger than cottage industries, and may have as many as 25 and more employees, many of whom are not family members. Often, the physical facility is located away from the home. The owner and employees must commute to their jobs.

Amish businesses are as efficient as non-Amish companies making the same products, despite the restrictions on electrical and gas attachments to public utilities. Gas lanterns provide light, and air and hydraulic or pneumatic power from diesel engines operate the machinery.

Mobile work crews are the third primary way in which Amish make a living beyond farming. Mobile work crews include industrial, commercial, and residential housing construction as well as silo building. Some are owned by the Amish, some are owned by the "English." Both Amish and "English" owners of businesses that require mobile work crews will provide "taxi" service for their Amish employees. Carpentry and woodworking are two of the most popular mobile work crew businesses. Roughly 35 percent of the Amish working off the farm are involved in carpentry and woodworking operations. Amish mobile work crews are popular with the "English" who are looking for quality in home construction and interior redecorating, such as kitchen cabinets.

The fourth type of non-farm employment for the Amish is related to the **tourist industry**, particularly employment in restaurants and hotels. The majority of the Amish employed in these businesses are single women. There are a few married Amish women working outside the home, but this is still fairly rare.

Amish women working in the tourist industry may be identified by the prayer coverings they wear. These prayer coverings are worn from the time they are little girls until they die. They are made of Swiss organdy material and usually are white. Amish women wear them at all times, or at least a bandanna or scarf to cover their head, especially when praying or in the presence of men other than their husbands.

It is possible to spot Amish businesses from the road without the benefit of any travel guide. Look for signs that are simple, hand lettered, and do not mention the word "Amish." A simple "rule of thumb" is that the fancier the sign, and the more the sign uses words like "Das," or "Amish," the greater the chance is that it is an "English"-owned business. The Amish keep their signs direct and simple, and you may need to look twice before you see it (so slow down). "Eggs for sale, but not on Sunday," is one example of an Amish sign.

Another way to identify an Amish business is to ask around. For example, if you are interested in having furniture custom made, you will have to ask for recommendations for shops, as well as directions to the business.

Despite the diversity of Amish businesses, they do have one thing in common. The services and products provided through Amish micro-enterprises involves more hand labor than an "English" business of the same type. In this sense, Amish businesses resemble the same investment in manual labor that is necessary to run a farm.

8

The *Future*

"Our community of four church districts gained
39 new members last year…
We had 23 new babies…
The other 16 new members moved in from
Maryland, New York, and Lebanon County, PA."

The Budget, January 1994

⌒The Future⌒

O ver the years, many "experts" predicted that the Amish would not survive. As these so-called forecasters looked at how rapidly American society was changing, and how quickly it transformed from an agricultural society of small towns and villages to an industrial society of sprawling metropolises and endless suburbs, it was hard to imagine that any group resisting this trend would last very long. Other traditional groups around the world have been threatened with extinction or have already vanished as their countries entered the industrial era. Why should the Amish be any different? The industrial revolution and modernization was likened to a giant tidal wave that would sweep over the top of so "fragile" a culture as the Amish.

The Amish have proved these prognosticators wrong. Why? First, there was a false assumption among these forecasters that *modern* and *technology* mean the same thing. However, there is an *alternative* definition of *modern* that fits well in an American society that has always been more accommodating to religious freedom and diverse peoples and lifestyles. This alternative definition says that being modern is *the ability of people to live the life they want to live.* In this sense, it can be argued that the Amish are more modern than almost everyone else in American society. After all, their world is one of two cultures: one that is their religious beliefs and their way of life; and the other that is the world of the "English" that surrounds them and provides both support and challenge to Amish ways.

Young Amish men and women are not baptized until they are adults and they choose to do so of their own free will. This is in the tradition of Anabaptism. There is plenty of exposure to the "English" world, and a great deal of it comes from the constant flow of tourists to areas where the Amish have settled. Yet, as noted earlier, the vast majority of boys and girls born to Amish parents decide to be baptized into the Amish faith, and only a few drop out after they are baptized.

Second, many people see the Amish as a *non-changing* society. In fact, some "English" write and give speeches about the Amish as a traditional society that never or rarely changes. They falsely idealize the Amish and hold up the Amish as an example of the right way to live, and criticize contemporary American lifestyles as "too fast," with "too many chemicals," with "too much technology," and so on, and so on. There is nothing wrong with worrying about present conditions and future directions of American society, but not at the cost of inaccurate information about the Amish. These critics idealize the Amish and often behave like overbearing parents, believing that it is their duty to protect the Amish from the rest of the "English." They give those who read and listen to their proclamations the incorrect assumption that the Amish are like a special species of animal whose habitat has now been threatened and will soon become extinct. This is hardly the case. *The strength of the Amish has been their own ability, over 300 plus years, to change without losing their sense of identity and history.* Two examples will illustrate just how this has been accomplished.

First, the Amish successfully relocated from Europe to North America. Despite severe persecution and discrimination, the Amish (and their Anabaptist predecessors) survived in the hostile environment of Europe and were able to "pull up stakes" and move into the frontier areas of the New World. Since then, the Amish have successfully established new communities throughout North America. Since 1900, the number of Amish has grown from an estimated population of 5,000 to over 200,000 today. Even as recently as 1979, the population of the Amish was about 85,000, a figure which more than doubled in less than 25 years. Population increase of this magnitude is hardly a sign of a society becoming extinct. In fact, it is a clear indicator of success and resiliency during a century that has witnessed a tremendous

Are Amish traditional or modern? If modern means having the freedom to consciously choose the way one wants to live, then the Amish are modern. If modern means possessing and using the latest in technology, then they are not. What does the reader think?

transformation in the greater "English" society surrounding the Amish.

Second, for three hundred plus years, the Amish have debated the virtues of adopting the new technologies of the time. One by one they have made decisions about the latest inventions and new ways of doing things, and established within their *Ordnung* whether or not each was appropriate to their lifestyle and religious values. Some technologies were rejected almost completely, such as television. Others could be used only under certain circumstances, such as riding in a car but without owning or driving a motor vehicle. Still others are being redesigned so that they can be adapted to the Amish way of life, such as bulk milk tanks run by diesel engines or a solar panel to charge the batteries to power the turn signals and lights on a buggy. Others were accepted entirely, such as battery-powered flashlights and calculators. In each case, the decision was made on the basis of what it means to be Amish and live according to the Amish version of Christianity.

Would this innovation weaken faith and values, or would it not make any difference whatsoever? These debates represent a dynamic, living, and functional culture.

The Amish are no different from every other society on this planet. Life will always present challenges, and change offers opportunities to renew the spirit of a culture, or to lose vitality, wither, and, eventually, die. History is filled with cultures long since dead. History also contains a wealth of success stories. The Amish are an example of a culture that chose to be separate and different, and in the midst of the great changes of industrialization and urbanization surrounding them, to maintain their vitality by constantly examining the impact of outside influences on their way of life.

There is no doubt that new and unforeseen challenges lie ahead for the Amish as the next century approaches. For the immediate future, some have already arrived. Here are three examples of trends in Amish society that may create new challenges.

One of the most important trends over the past 40 years has been the increasing number of husbands who make their living by working in factories and by running their own businesses. This trend away from farming presents several challenges to the Amish. The **first** challenge will be the size of Amish families. Children are valued not only as a gift from God, but also for the help they provide on the farm. Scientists who study population have found that the size of an Amish family is smaller when the husband works in a non-farm job. Will family planning become more widely accepted among the Amish? At present, birth control is against the *Ordnung*. Will this change for some church districts? A **second** challenge is to continue to find job opportunities for young men, especially as they become adults, get married, and start families. This is a very big challenge when one considers how rapidly Amish society has grown. Related to this is a **third** challenge, which is to find new places to settle as the population of the Amish continues to expand. Farmland is getting expensive everywhere, and in many areas where the best agricultural land is located, urban developments are encroaching. Even if most or all of the Amish breadwinners in a new settlement do not take up agriculture in order to make a living, it is still true that the Amish desire to live in rural locations, and to live near enough to each other so as to be able to communicate on a face-to-face basis. As land becomes prohibitively expensive, it becomes more difficult to find suitable locations for farming and for a rural based lifestyle.

A second important trend has been an internal division of the Amish into relatively more conservative and more progressive groups. Will there be more schisms in the future? And what will be the issues that encourage new fellowships of Amish to form? Will there be disagreements over the adoption of new technologies, or family planning, or some other unforeseen point of contention?

The third trend concerns tourists. Tourists will keep coming to visit Amish country, and their numbers are increasing every year. When it comes to tourists, the question is simple: How much is enough? Will there be a time when tourism so overwhelms an area, that it is no longer perceived by the Amish as a place where they can lead their way of life and raise their children in the Amish faith?

Where is the balance between the right of Americans to travel freely, and the right of all individuals to live according to their values? The answer may not lie in restricting the number of tourists who flock to Amish areas, but on the ability of tourists to understand the history, values, and religion of the Amish, and respect all of the people in the area where they are visiting.

This may appear to be a "one-way street." As a student in an Amish class at The Ohio State University once asked: "Why should we have to understand them, when they don't take the time to understand us?" Although this student's question may sound crass and intolerant, there is a little bit of good point in what he asked. People from different ways of life should learn to respect the ways of others. Promoting mutual understanding and respect is always better than encouraging intolerance, because intolerance leads to conflict. However, read-

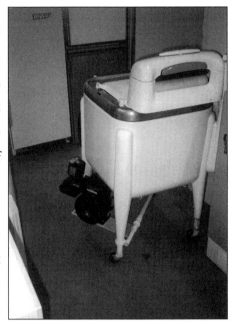

This gas-powered washing machine shows how technology can be adapted to cultural values.

ers should keep in mind that it is tourists who have traveled to Amish areas, and not the other way around. Tourists will have a richer and deeper learning experience if they understand enough about the history, religious values, and practices of the Amish to appreciate what they see, hear, and experience during their brief stays in Amish areas.

As the Amish man in the *Small Farmer's Journal* wrote: "If you admire our faith, strengthen yours." The authors of this book hope that they have taken readers on a brief but rewarding journey into the history, religion, and way of life of the Amish. By doing so, we believe that we have helped the readers develop a greater appreciation about why the Amish live the way they do, and thereby help readers appreciate their own lives and their own faith.

9

Making the

Most

of a Visit

To
An
Amish
Area

"We're having a nice Indian summer this week…
Farmers are busy with fall plowing
and rain would be welcome as the soil is dry."

The Budget, November 1992

Making the Most of a Visit

So many people visit areas where there are settlements of Amish that there is concern about these communities becoming "overrun" with tourists. Sometimes the crowded roads become the scene of a tragedy, such as an accident involving a buggy and an automobile, or an Amish person walking alongside the road or riding a bicycle who is struck by a car. Most of the hassles from tourists, however, come from the inconvenience of crowds. Some Amish avoid going to town to shop for groceries

This group of tourists is enjoying lunch at the home of an Amish family. In several Amish communities, Amish women operate restaurants out of their homes.

and other necessities during peak times of the day when the tourists are around. Local people who are not Amish also get tired of the constant stream of out-of-county license plates on cars, vans, and buses that disrupt the peace of their neighborhoods.

The primary way to visit an Amish area is by a motor vehicle. Most tourists stay less than a day, although in all the larger settlements, there is a growing supply of hotels and bed and breakfast operations. Of course, restaurants and tourist shops abound.

Compared to the smaller settlements, the Amish in the larger groupings are more visible. In places like the greater Holmes County community of northeast Ohio, the Lancaster County community area in southeast Pennsylvania, and the Elkhart/La-Grange County community area in northern Indiana, the Amish make up a sizable proportion of the local population. It is easier in these areas for tourists to get a sense that they have experienced and learned something about the Amish.

There are two basic rules for "making the most" out of a visit to an Amish area. **First**, making the most means that the trip should be **educational**. What is educational? *Educational means learning something new about the Amish and developing a deeper understanding about their religious values, and how these values are related to the way they live.*

Educational *does* mean that when tourists learn a little about the Amish, by doing so they are also able to reflect more deeply on their own lives. Educational also *means* a recognition that there is always more to learn and understand, not only about the Amish, but also about oneself.

Educational does *not* mean memorizing the minutiae of clothing styles, buggies, how the Amish farm, religious practices, and other aspects of their way of life, and then forgetting about the "bigger picture" of how the specifics are related to the history and heritage of Amish society. Educational does *not* mean looking at the Amish through a magnifying glass, searching for inconsistencies between values and the way someone who is Amish actually lives, and then arrogantly judging all Amish to be "hypocritical."

Second, making the most out of a trip means treating the Amish and the "English" who live in the area with respect. It is their home and their back yard that tourists are visiting. Tourists should keep in mind that the Amish have developed a lifestyle based on the notion of being separate from the world. This does not mean living a life isolated from the world. It does mean leading a life that adheres to Amish religious values. They may be different in many ways from the rest of American society, but no one, including the Amish, wants to be treated like they are animals in a zoo. Tourists who are rude, who are too intrusive by taking pictures of the Amish (which goes against their interpretation of the Second Commandment), and who tailgate too closely to buggies and honk their horns because they are impatient with the slow pace, are not only impolite, but have not brought to their trip an approach that allows them to make it an educational experience.

A recent survey of tourists in the greater Holmes County community conducted by the authors found that tourists complained most about buggies on the road. The authors were both bemused and confused about why someone would visit an Amish area and then complain because the Amish were in their way.

Listed below are tips that we, the authors, believe will enhance the readers' visit to Amish areas.

Tips for Driving in Amish Areas:

Try to remember that the Amish still operate mostly in a pre-automobile society. Their principal mode of travel is the horse and buggy. Too many tourists bring the skills on which they have

Even during the day, buggies may be hard to see, especially if skies are overcast.

learned to survive when driving in the big city to their sojourn through Amish country. **Slow down and forget about city driving styles.**

The Amish are often located in areas with rolling hills. There are many blind spots on the roads. Many of the back roads are made of gravel. Cars, vans, and buses that travel at high speeds can come up too fast on the back of buggies, and with serious consequences. Even the fastest horse is slow compared to a car. A car traveling at 55 miles per hour and coming fast upon a horse-drawn vehicle 500 feet ahead, traveling at only 5 miles per hour, has a mere 6 seconds to react.

Passing buggies on the road should be done with great care and with the same caution that one should always apply when passing slower moving cars and trucks. Wait for a good view of the road ahead and be careful not to make too much dust, or kick up gravel stones which make the horses jittery. Horses are not machines. They are intelligent animals and God's creatures, and can react to loud noises and other distractions from passing vehicles in ways that put those in the buggy at risk to an accident.

Remember that Amish buggy drivers can make the same mistakes as "English" automobile drivers. Sometimes they decide to cross a busy highway when they should not, or have other lapses in judgment that can cause an accident. Always drive defensively in Amish areas!

A slower pace has an added advantage because it provides the tourist a greater chance to enjoy a drive in the country and to see and experience more about the Amish. However, it must be kept in mind that sight-seeing is best left to the passengers in a vehicle. The driver needs to pay attention to motor vehicle, buggy, and pedestrian traffic on the road. One good idea is to *rotate the driving responsibilities* so that everyone has an opportunity to enjoy the ride and the scenery.

Many Amish have adopted the orange slow-moving vehicle sign on the back of their buggies, and have attached reflective tape on the backs and sides in order to make their vehicles more visible. However, on cloudy days and late afternoon hours, buggies may still be difficult to see. Tourists should always be alert.

Locating Amish Businesses:

Often tourists have heard about an Amish-owned business, such as one that makes furniture or baskets. They want to stop by, visit, examine the goods, and perhaps purchase an item or place a custom order. These Amish-owned businesses are generally located on back country roads, not in the center of tourist towns. Too many tourists become easily frustrated by their inability to locate an Amish business right away. Tourists who come to Amish areas in search of Amish businesses should take a different philosophical approach to shopping—get off the "main drag," slow down, drive safely, and enjoy the scenery along the way!

The Chambers of Commerce in most areas where the Amish live can provide a list of tourist businesses. In the larger settlement areas, these Chambers of Commerce include: 1) Ashland, Coshocton, Holmes, Stark, Tuscarawas, and Wayne Counties in Ohio; 2) Lancaster and Chester Counties in Pennsylvania; 3) Elkhart and LaGrange Counties in Indiana; and 4) Geauga County in Ohio. There may be special directories of Amish-owned and operated businesses. Do not be afraid to ask directions to these businesses. Chambers of Commerce can supply maps of the area, but sometimes back roads of rural areas are not clearly marked. Stop and ask directions from Amish people along the way. They will usually be glad to assist you in finding a certain address. Some Amish may be reserved around strangers. A smile, a courteous request for directions, and the universal magic words of "please" and "thank you," remain the ingredients to a productive request for assistance.

Some Amish-owned businesses are visible from the road, with signs that advertise the availability of handwoven baskets, fresh produce, and baked goods. Some tourists may feel shy or uncomfortable about stopping at these places. As one tourist said: "If I stop, I'll feel an obligation to buy something. So, I don't stop." There is no reason to feel that way. Shopping is shopping, whether it be in an "English"-owned or an Amish-owned business. Tourists should only buy what they value. The Amish appreciate a shopper who is not frivolous. In addition, these roadside businesses provide an opportunity for short but direct experiences with the Amish.

Auctions:

In most Amish areas, there are regular auctions of farm animals, horses, and other commodities. In Amish areas, there often are special auctions that raise money for charitable causes. There are lots of sights and sounds and smells at any auction. These provide excellent opportunities for tourists to learn about farming and rural lifestyles, and perhaps to buy a handmade quilt or piece of furniture. Chambers of Commerce usually have information on the location and time of auctions. Also, look for posted signs in local shops, or ask the shop owner.

Tourist Businesses:

A number of restaurants and cheese-making places can also be educational. Tourist businesses can vary in their authenticity, however. Remember, when it comes to tourist businesses, the word "Amish" is used to promote everything from "A to Z." Some have little or no connection to the Amish, except that their business signs include a picture of a buggy or of an Amish man with suspenders and a broad-brimmed hat. The Amish, however, do not permit the use of the name "Amish" to sell products. A simple "rule of thumb" to follow is that the word "Amish" in the name of the business means that it is *not Amish*.

Here are three excellent places in the largest Amish settlements that will help readers expand their knowledge about the Amish (and related groups, such as the Mennonites).

In the greater **Holmes County community**, there is the "Behalt" Mennonite Information Center. This center is located on County Road 77 about one mile northeast of Berlin, Ohio. The Behalt is a 265-foot cyclorama describing the history, culture, and lifestyle of the Amish, Mennonites, and Hutterites. There is a guided presentation of the historical events that helped to shape these branches of Anabaptism. It takes about one hour and gives the reasons for the distinctive characteristics of the Amish, conservative Mennonites, and Hutterites. There is also a video about Holmes County and the Amish, as well as a gift and book store. The author's Amish friends have made favorable comments about its value for understanding the Amish. For more information, call 330-893-3192.

In the **Lancaster, Pennsylvania, community** readers can visit the Mennonite Information Center at 2209 Millstream Road. It is located southeast of Lancaster City. From State Route 30, turn south onto Millstream Road. The Mennonite Information Center includes movies and exhibits about Anabaptism, plus guided tours on Amish (and Mennonite) culture. The Mennonite Information Center can be reached at 717-299-0954. Also in the Lancaster area is The People's Place. The People's Place shows a 30-minute documentary about the Amish, using three screens and nine projectors, plus an exhibit area featuring many aspects of Amish culture. The People's Place is located on State Route 340 in the village of Intercourse, PA. The telephone number is 800-390-8436.

Visitors to the **Elkhart/LaGrange County, Indiana, community area** should stop at the Menno-Hof Center in Shipshewana. It is located just north of the intersection of Indiana State Route 5 and U.S. Route 20. The Menno-Hof Center provides multimedia presentations on the history of the Anabaptists in Europe that includes replicas of a dungeon where Anabaptists were imprisoned and tortured and the inside of a typical sailing ship that brought them to the New World. The center offers 24 different programs featuring the history, beliefs, and way of life of Amish, Mennonite, and Hutterite groups. Their phone number is 261-768-4117.

Tips for a Windshield Tour of Amish Areas:

When driving on the back roads in an Amish area, there are certain things that can be observed. Most of these represent the "material" or outward aspects of Amish culture. The authors would like to remind readers that these outward signs are more than mere curiosities; they are based on the history and religious values of the Amish. Here is what the tourist may be able to see from the windshield of a motor vehicle:

Houses

- Look for houses with no electric lines.
- Look for a grandfather or *dawdy haus* next to or attached to the main house.
- Observe the location of the house in relation to the barn and other farm buildings. Where is the garden? Is there a swing for the children? The arrangement of the house, farm buildings, and other things represent decisions about how work in the home and on the farm is to be accomplished.
- Some Amish homes have roadside stands for selling baked goods, fruits, and vegetables, or have handwoven baskets and other crafts available for sale. Signs may not be obvious, so look closely.

Farms

- Look for farm work, such as plowing and cultivating the fields, harvesting corn, oats, wheat, and other grain crops, and hauling hay and wheat.

The dawdy haus, which is attached or next to the main house, is one sign that the family living there is Amish.

- The long one-story buildings are for raising broilers (chickens for meat).
- Most farms have a herd of dairy cows, plus chickens and other birds. A few will have peacocks, emus, llamas, and other unusual birds and animals. Also, look for buggy horses and workhorses, either grazing in the fields or working.

Buggies

- Buggies come in different sizes and shapes. Styles can vary from one settlement of Amish to another. Within the larger settlements, buggies of more conservative Amish are less fancy than the buggies of more progressive Amish. In addition, there are buggies for hauling things, "souped up" buggies of teenage Amish, family buggies, etc.

Along the Road

- Most Amish schools are one-room structures with outdoor toilets, swings, and a baseball field. These schools are located within easy walking distance for all the children.
- Telephone booths or "shanties" along the road are usually private phones used by the Amish only (or mostly) for business purposes.
- Amish-owned businesses along the road may have only a small sign indicating the type of business, such as furniture, bulk food, quilts, etc., and there is rarely any mention of the word "Amish" in the name of the business.

Enjoy Your Visit and Drive Carefully.

10

Recipes and
Remedies

"We had a pizza and ice cream supper Wednesday
evening. Yesterday we were at the neighbors for dinner,
now tonight we are invited to the Bylers for supper.
If this keeps up, we'll be well fed."

. . . .

"I would encourage everyone not to fall for all those
healing claims on medicine, etc. God is our healer.
I believe he gave herbs to use, but when so many strange
things have to be done, then I question it.
Read the book of James. A pretty good guide for us all."

The Budget, February 1997

⌒Recipes and Remedies⌒

Recipes

For generations the Amish have been known for their good home cooking. That is no less true today, so we have asked our Amish friends to share some of their recipes with us. We hope you enjoy them as much as we do.

Date Cake Pudding

1 c. cut-up dates	$1\frac{1}{2}$ c. flour
1 tsp. baking soda	1 c. brown sugar
1 Tbsp. oleo	1 egg
$\frac{3}{4}$ c. boiling water	1 tsp. vanilla
	$\frac{1}{2}$ c. nuts

Mix first four ingredients and let stand until cool. Add flour, sugar, egg, vanilla, and nuts. Bake at 350° for 30 min. Serve with whipped topping, caramel sauce, or bananas.

Caramel Sauce

$\frac{1}{2}$ c. butter	2 egg yolks
1 c. water	$2\frac{1}{2}$ Tbsp. cornstarch
1 c. brown sugar	$1\frac{1}{2}$ c. milk

Melt butter, add sugar, and stir well. Add water and boil 5 min. Mix cornstarch, egg yolks, and milk. Add to above mixture. Cook until it boils. Cool before serving.

Shoo-Fly Pie

Syrup:

1 c. molasses (dark Karo)

$1/2$ c. brown sugar

2 eggs—beaten

butter)

1 c. hot water

1 tsp. soda dissolved in hot water

Crumbs:

2 c. flour

$1/4$ c. brown sugar

$1/3$ c. shortening (lard or

$1/2$ tsp. nutmeg

1 tsp. cinnamon

$1/2$ tsp. salt

Mix syrup all together. Pour into 2 unbaked pie shells. Mix crumbs all together until crumbly. Sprinkle over syrup—divided in 2 shells. Bake at 400° for 10 min. Reduce oven to 350°, bake until set—about 40-50 min.

Date Pudding

$1/2$ c. sugar

2 Tbsp. flour (heaping)

2 eggs (separated)

1 tsp. baking powder

$1/2$ c. milk

1 lb. dates (chopped)

$1/2$ c. nuts (chopped)

Mix all above ingredients, except egg whites. Add beaten egg whites last. Bake in sprayed 8" x 8" pan, at 350° for 30 min. Break into pieces and mix with whipped cream or whipped topping.

Pie Crust

20 c. Flaky Crust pastry flour	4 tsp. baking powder
1 can butter flavored Crisco	4 tsp. salt

Mix together to form crumbs. May be stored in refrigerator. When ready to use, add 1 Tbsp. vinegar to 8 oz. water and use this to moisten crumbs. For a double crust pie use 2½ c. of crumbs and about ½ c. of cold water.

From Verna Miller

Pie Dough

3 c. lard	1 egg
9 c. flour	1 Tbsp. vinegar
¼ tsp. salt	1¼ c. cold water

Mix together flour, lard, and salt. In a separate bowl mix egg, vinegar, and water. Add to flour mixture. Makes 10 crusts.

Red Raspberry Cream Pie

1 qt. red raspberries	½ tsp. salt
1 qt. water	2 Tbsp. clear jel
2 c. sugar	(or cornstarch)
	soaked in ¾ c. water

Soak raspberries in water for 5 min. Mix sugar, salt, and clear jel and stir well. Add to fruit mixture and cook until thickened. Add 1 box raspberry jello. Add one 8 oz. carton of Cool Whip. Mix well and put in two baked pie shells. Top with whipped cream or whipped topping.

From Maudie Raber

Raisin Pie

1 box raisins	2 c. brown sugar
2 qts. water	1/2 c. white sugar

Simmer slowly for 2 hours. Add a little water to 3/4 c. clear jel (or cornstarch) and add to the raisins and simmer until thickened. Add 1/2 tsp. salt. Makes 3 or 4 pies, depending on size of pan. Double crust. Bake 20 min. at 400°.

Peanut Butter Cream Pie

2 c. milk	2 egg yolks
1/2 c. sugar	1 Tbsp. butter
2 Tbsp. flour	1/2 tsp. salt
3 Tbsp. cornstarch	1 tsp. vanilla

Scald 1 1/2 c. milk in top of double boiler. Combine sugar, flour, and cornstarch. Stir in remaining 1/2 c. milk and egg yolks. Add this mixture to hot milk and cook until thickened. Remove from heat. Add butter, salt, and vanilla. Let cool and pour into baked pie shell. Top with whipped cream or whipped topping. Sprinkle peanut butter crumbs on top.

Peanut Butter Crumbs

Mix 1/3 c. peanut butter with 3/4 c. powdered sugar. Line bottom of baked pie shell with crumbs (save a few for the top). Pour in the cream filling and top with whipped cream. Sprinkle remaining crumbs on top.

Maudie's Favorite Holiday Cookies

2 c. sugar	Pinch salt
1 c. shortening	1 c. buttermilk
3 eggs	2 tsp. baking powder
4$^{1}/_{2}$ c. Gold Medal flour	1 tsp. soda

Mix all together and use enough flour to make a thick dough so it can be rolled. If making drop cookies use a little less flour and drop by tablespoons. Refrigerate overnight. Bake on ungreased cookie sheet 10 min. at 375°. Do not bake until brown. Ice with caramel icing.

Caramel Icing

$^{1}/_{4}$ c. butter	1 c. brown sugar
$^{1}/_{4}$ c. Carnation milk	

Mix and add powdered sugar to thicken to spreading consistency.

From Maudie Raber

Molasses & Ginger Cookies

¹/₄ c. molasses	¹/₂ tsp. ginger
1 stick oleo	¹/₂ tsp. ground cloves
1 egg	¹/₂ tsp. salt
1 c. sugar	1 tsp. cinnamon
2 c. flour	2 tsp. baking soda

Cream oleo and sugar, then mix in all other ingredients. Place in freezer for 15 min. or refrigerator for 1 hour. Roll into balls; cover with sugar. Bake on greased cookie sheet 8 to 10 min. at 340°.

Chewy Oatmeal Cookies

1¹/₂ c. margarine	3 c. flour
4 eggs	1 tsp. salt
3 c. brown sugar	1¹/₂ tsp. baking soda
2 tsp. vanilla	2 tsp. cinnamon
	4 c. cooking oats

In a large bowl cream margarine, eggs, brown sugar, and vanilla. Add dry ingredients. Mix and add oats last. Drop on ungreased cookie sheet 2 inches apart. Bake at 350°. *Do not overbake.*

Creme Filling

2 beaten egg whites

1 Tbsp. vanilla

3 c. powdered sugar

1¼ c. Crisco

¾ c.
    marshmallow creme
    (optional)

Beat egg whites, vanilla, and sugar and add Crisco. Beat until smooth. Put creme between two cookies.

Soft Oatmeal Cookies

1 c. quick-cooking oats

2 c. boiling water

3 Tbsp. margarine

Cook this and pour over:

²/₃ c. brown sugar

1½ tsp. salt

Dissolve in ⅓ c. warm water:

2 Tbsp. dry yeast

1 Tbsp. white sugar

Mix above ingredients and add:

5 c. bread flour, a cup at a time.

Let rise once, punch down and roll out. Cut with cookie cutter. Bake at 350° until lightly brown.

Sweet Rolls

Combine:

1 c. milk (scalded)	½ c. sugar
1½ tsp. salt	½ c. shortening

Dissolve:

1 Tbsp. sugar	2 Tbsp. yeast
1 c. lukewarm water	

Combine the above and add:

2 eggs (beaten)

2 tsp. vanilla

Beat well. Gradually add 7 cups all-purpose flour. Knead lightly. Let rise 2 hours or until double in size. Work down and let rise again.

Divide dough into 2 equal parts. Roll out. Brush with melted butter and sprinkle with sugar and cinnamon. Roll up and cut into 1½" slices; put in pan and let rise until light, about 1 hour.

Bake at 350° for 25 minutes. Cool before frosting.

Caramel Frosting for Rolls

½ c. butter	1¾ to 2 c.
1 c. brown sugar	powdered sugar
	¼ c. rich milk

Melt butter and sugar; boil 2 minutes, stirring constantly. Add milk and bring to boil. Cool to lukewarm. Add powdered sugar until stiff enough to spread. If too stiff, add a little hot water.

From Erma Beachy

Honey Wheat Bread

In a large bowl combine:

½ c. honey	1 Tbsp. salt
⅓ c. oil	2 c. boiling water

Add 3 cups whole wheat flour; cook to lukewarm.

In a small bowl combine:

1¾ Tbsp. yeast

½ tsp. sugar

1 c. warm water

Let set until foamy.

Combine the above and add 5 to 6 cups flour (for best results use high gluten flour).

Mix and turn onto floured board. Knead until smooth and elastic, about 8 to 10 minutes.

Place in a greased bowl, turning to grease top. Cover. Let rise in warm place, free from draft, until double in bulk, about 1¼ hours.

Punch dough down, divide into 4 equal parts, cover and let rise 10 minutes. Shape into loaves. Place in 4 greased 8¼" x 4½" x 2½" pans. Cover.

Let rise until double in bulk, about 1 hour.

Bake at 350° for about 25 minutes.

Buns

Combine:

1/4 c. warm water	1 tsp. sugar
1 pkg. yeast (1 Tbsp.)	

Let stand 5 minutes.

Mix:

1 tsp. salt	1/4 c. shortening
1 egg (beaten)	2 c. very hot water

Combine the above and add 6 cups bread flour.

Stir well. This will be a soft dough. Refrigerate overnight. Next morning work dough into Brown & Serve Rolls. Bake at 425° for 10 to 15 minutes.

Granola

6 c. quick-cooking oats	1/2 c. wheat germ
1 c. flaked coconut	1/2 c. honey
1/2 c. wheat bran	1/2 c. brown sugar
2/3 c. oil	1 1/2 tsp. vanilla
2 Tbsp. water	1 1/2 tsp. maple flavoring
3/4 c. sliced almonds	

In a large bowl toss oats, almonds, coconut, wheat germ, and wheat bran. In a saucepan combine oil, brown sugar, honey, vanilla, maple flavoring, and water. Cook on low heat until warm and well mixed. Pour over cereal and mix until evenly coated. Pour into two 9" x 13" x 2" pans and bake at 275° for 50 to 60 min. Stir every 15 min. Cool. Store in an airtight container.

Grape-Nut Cereal

¹/₂ c. oleo	1 tsp. vanilla
1 c. brown sugar	1 tsp. maple flavoring
2 c. buttermilk	3 c. whole wheat flour
1 tsp. salt	1 c. wheat bran
1¹/₂ tsp. baking soda	

Mix and bake at 350° about 40 min. or until done. When cold, crumble into fine pieces and toast in a 300° oven until nicely browned. Stir every 15 min. Serve with milk and fruit. Store in an airtight container.

Mint Tea

1 gal. water

1 lg. handful green mint tea (about 1 pt.)

Bring water to boil. Add tea and turn heat off. Let stand 10 min. Take out leaves. Sugar or honey may be added. Serve hot or cold.

From Verna Miller

Potluck Potatoes

5 lb. potatoes cooked in skins

1 stick butter or oleo

2 cans cream of chicken soup

$^1\!/_2$ c. sour cream

$^1\!/_2$ c. Half & Half

$^1\!/_2$ lb. Velveeta cheese

Garlic salt, salt &

   pepper to taste

   Peel potatoes when cold and dice. Mix all ingredients together and bake 1 hour at 350°. Serves 25.

From Verna Miller

Barbecued Beans

1 lb. ground beef

$^1\!/_2$ tsp. salt

1 can (1 lb. 12 oz.) pork & beans

1 Tbsp. Worcestershire sauce

$^1\!/_4$ tsp. Tabasco

$^1\!/_2$ c. onion (chopped)

$^1\!/_4$ tsp. pepper

$^1\!/_2$ c. catsup

2 Tbsp. vinegar

   Brown beef and onions and pour off fat. Add all other ingredients; mix well. Bake at 350° for 30 min.

From Erma Beachy

Cole Slaw

3 lb. cabbage (chopped)

1 green pepper (chopped)

2 carrots (chopped)

1½ c. sugar

1 c. vinegar

1 c. vegetable oil

1 Tbsp. celery seed

Mix oil, vinegar, celery seed, and sugar and bring to a boil. Pour over cabbage mixture and toss to coat. Store in an airtight container. Will keep in refrigerator for a month.

Wedding Chicken

Roll chicken pieces in Runion's Crumbs (purchased from Dan Kline, 3835 TR 374, Millersburg, OH 44654). Brown in oil and put in roasting pan. Cover. Bake 1½ hours at 350°.

From Verna Miller

Baked Hamburger

1 lb. ground beef

½ c. bread or cracker crumbs

2 eggs

½ c. milk

1 small onion

Salt and pepper to taste

Form patties. Brown in skillet and put in casserole.

Combine:

½ c. catsup

2 Tbsp. mustard

¾ tsp. salt

½ c. sugar

2 Tbsp. vinegar

½ c. water

Pour over patties and bake 1 hour at 350°.

From Erma Beachy

Pizza Casserole

2 lb. hamburger

1 can cream of mushroom soup

1 can mushrooms w/liquid (4 oz.)

1 pt. pizza sauce

pepperoni

8 oz. noodles

$1/2$ green pepper

1 medium onion

$1/4$ tsp. oregano

mozzarella cheese

Cook noodles. Brown hamburger and add green pepper, onion, oregano, soup, mushrooms, and pizza sauce. Put noodles in casserole and cover with meat mixture. Add a layer of pepperoni, then mozzarella, and end with more pepperoni. Bake $3/4$ hour at 350°.

Home Remedies

All agricultural societies have collected "folk remedies" that are passed down from generation to generation. We have included a number of home remedies that represent examples of the collected wisdom of generations of Amish and that illustrate their agricultural and German/Swiss roots.

These are not recommended to the reader as something they should try without the approval of their doctor. They are included here only for information about some of the non-medical health practices of the Amish.

For Gallstones

Juices of 2 lemons

1 Tbsp. cream of tartar

1 Tbsp. Epsom salt

$^1/_2$ pt. warm water

Do not boil.

For Yellow Jaundice in Babies

1 egg yolk to 8 oz. milk

Mix with 1 Tbsp. Karo syrup.

Heat, then strain and add boiled water as desired.

Wintergreen Liniment

2 oz. wintergreen oil

12 oz. rubbing alcohol

16 - 20 aspirin

Shake well.

For Rheumatism or Neuritis

1 lb. powdered sugar

4 Tbsp. Epsom salt

5 tsp. cream of tartar

2 oz. tartaric acid

Mix together.

For Bee Stings

Bathe in apple cider vinegar for 15 min. Jewelweed juice is also good.

For Poison Ivy

1 tsp. quince seeds

$1/2$ c. very warm water

Let stand overnight. It will thicken.

Spring Tonic

Sulfur and molasses in the spring to thin the blood.

To build up blood drink lots of sassafras tea.

Salve for Bleeding Piles

Take 2 handfuls of peach leaves and fry in 2 tablespoons lard until leaves are black and the lard is dark.

Mix 1 tablespoon butter, 2 teaspoons turpentine, and a pinch of salt to make salve.

High Blood Pressure

Eat apples, grapes, cranberries or their juice.

Eat a small amount of honey at each meal.

Ulcers in Stomach

Drink lots of cabbage juice.

Kidney and Bladder Problems

Steep 1 teaspoon of watermelon seeds in 1 pt. of water.

Fainting

A drink of vinegar is a sure cure.

Something in Your Eye

When you get something in your eye put a flaxseed in your eye and it will bring out the dirt.

For General Good Health

Jogg (shake) in a jug

6 cups grape juice

6 cups apple juice

2 cups apple cider

Eczema

Make a tea of yellowdock (1 tsp. to 2 cups hot water).

Kidney Problems

Dry corn silks from sweet corn. Soak them in water to make a tea. Also the flowers, roots, and leaves from dandelions can be dried and used to make a tea.

11

Recommended Reading

An Amish woman reflects on criticism…
"We should not be surprised,
as a different approach to us was eventual,
for as the saying goes, 'What goes up must come down.'
Our way of life has been held up and glamorized
so much in the past decade, or more,
and a lot from exaggerated untruths.
It stands to reason that we
may also come crashing down by untruths, too."

⌒Recommended Reading⌒

There are many excellent books about the Amish. They provide the reader with accurate information, and give the reader a greater understanding of the Amish and their culture. Those listed below have been read by the authors, and represent our personal recommendations.

Diane Donnermeyer and Joseph Donnermeyer. *An Amish Winter Visit* (a book for children). Columbus, Ohio: Tater Ridge Press.

Joseph F. Donnermeyer, George M. Kreps, and Marty W. Kreps. 1999. *Lessons for Living: A Practical Approach to Daily Life from the Amish Community*. Walnut Creek, Ohio: Carlisle Press.

John Hostetler. 1989. *Amish Roots: A Treasury of History, Wisdom, and Lore*. Baltimore, Maryland: The Johns Hopkins University Press.

John Hostetler. 1993. *Amish Society (4th edition)*. Baltimore, Maryland: The Johns Hopkins University Press.

John Hostetler and Gertrude Enders Huntington. 1992. *Amish Children: Education in the Family, School, and Community (2nd edition)*. Fort Worth: Harcourt Brace Jovanovich College Publishers.

David Kline. 1990. *Great Possessions: An Amish Farmer's Journal*. Wooster, Ohio: The Wooster Book Company

Donald B. Kraybill. 2001 (revised edition). *The Riddle of Amish Culture*. Baltimore, Maryland: The Johns Hopkins University Press.

Donald B. Kraybill (ed.). 1993. *The Amish and the State*. Baltimore, Maryland: The Johns Hopkins University Press.

Donald B. Kraybill and Marc A. Olshan (eds.). 1994. *The Amish Struggle with Modernity*. Hanover, New Hampshire: University Press of New England.

Steven Nolt. 2004 (revised & updated). *A History of the Amish*. Intercourse, Pennsylvania: Good Books.

William I. Schreiber. 1962 (reprinted in 1990). *Our Amish Neighbors*. Wooster, Ohio: The College of Wooster.

John Wasilchick. 1991. *Amish Life: A Portrait of Plain Living*. New York: Crescent Books.

Paton Yoder. 1991. *Tradition and Transition: Amish Mennonites and Old Order Amish 1800-1900*. Scottdale, Pennsylvania: Herald Press.

Stories about the Amish are contained in three series of books. The first set was written by Joseph W. Yoder, whose mother was raised by an Amish woman. The titles are *Rosanna of the Amish* and *Rosanna's Boys*, and are published by Choice Productions of Harrisonburg, Virginia. The second set was written by Mary Christner Borntrager, who was raised Amish and later on attended Eastern Mennonite University in Harrisonburg, Virginia. Her many books are novels about the challenges of growing up in Amish culture. The titles include *Ellie, Rebecca, Rachel, Daniel,* and *Reuben*. They are published by Herald Press of Scottdale,

Pennsylvania. The third set was written by Martin and Susan Hochstetler, an Amish couple, about their experiences living in Ohio and Montana and the Canadian province of British Columbia. The titles of the books are *Cabin Life on the Kootenai, Farm Life in the Hills,* and *Life on the Edge of the Wilderness.* These Hochstetler books may be a little hard to obtain because they are not sold at "English" bookstores. However, stores specializing in Anabaptist literature may have copies for purchase.

⌒Index⌒

This book has been printed by Carlisle Printing of Walnut Creek, Ohio. It is owned and operated by Marcus Wengerd. Marcus is a member of the Amish and he represents one of the many young Amish entrepreneurs who are developing new businesses apart from farming while at the same time remaining faithful to their Amish traditions. He and the employees of his company are dedicated to producing a quality product for their customers. They are mostly self-taught in the printing business and continue to expand their knowledge about publishing.

Other Books by the Authors

Diane and Joe Donnermeyer
Illustrated by Marty Husted ▶

In *An Amish Winter Visit*, two children from the city are introduced to the beliefs and values of the Amish through their newfound Amish friends.

▲ Joseph F. Donnermeyer, George M. Kreps and Marty W. Kreps

Lessons for Living is must reading for anyone looking for a new and profound sense of community in this new century.

Available through **Tater Ridge Press**
4813 Teter Court • Columbus, Ohio 43220
614-451-9830